Large Creatures

Large Creatures

Creatures can be large in different ways...

There are undisputed heavyweights, such as blue whales
and hippopotamuses, there are the thick-skinned pachyderms
(elephants and rhinoceroses), heavy lumbering animals,
fierce titans or good-natured juggernauts.

Some of the large creatures are majestic in their size:
the fearsome Siberian tiger, the red deer with its huge antlers
(weighing between 15 and 20 kilograms and measuring up to 1.5 metres),
and the albatross whose huge wings prevent it from walking
but give it a majestic, gliding flight.

Then there are the tall and slender animals: the elegant giraffe
that nibbles delicately at treetops some 6 metres above the ground,
or the 8-metre long anaconda that slips silently along the banks
of the Orinoco River to embrace its prey in its deadly coils.

The animal kingdom includes all kinds of large and heavy creatures,
from huge flightless birds – the ostrich weighs in at 120 kilograms –
to tiny baby leatherback turtles that weigh around 30 grams at birth and
grow to be marine giants and one of the world's heaviest reptiles –
up to 1.9 metres long and weighing 400 kilograms!

- Relentlessly hunted for their ivory tusks, **elephants** are now an endangered species...6
- The largest dolphins, **orcs** are the scourge of the seas...10 - With their gliding flight **condors** are the lords of the air...12 - With their magnificent antlers, **red deer** are the aristocrats of the forest...14 - Today **bison** are the heaviest mammals in Europe...18
- Like slow-moving tanks on legs, **giant tortoises** seem to have emerged from the depths of time...20 - Their graceful leaps belie the fact that **whales** weigh as much as a herd of elephants...22 - Lords of the Arctic, **polar bears** are the world's largest carnivores...26 - They may not be able to fly, but **ostriches** are fast on their feet...28
- With their fearsome fangs and claws, **tigers** are terrifying and fascinating creatures...30
- Siren or sea cow, **manatees** are gentle, harmless creatures...34 - Renowned for swallowing their victims whole, **giant snakes** have always been the object of great fascination...36 - In spite of their great size, **gorillas** are shy and retiring creatures...38
- On their huge wings, **albatrosses** glide high above the cold southern oceans...42
- Much maligned, **giant clams** are in fact real 'pearls'...44 - Hunted for their highly prized horns, **rhinoceroses** are the last survivors of a prehistoric age...46 - Despite being the largest members of the shark family **whale sharks** are non-aggressive plankton-eaters...50 - One hump or two, **camels** are faithful companions in the desert...52 - From tiny hatchlings to marine giants, **leatherback turtles** fight a constant battle for survival...54 - With their bald heads and long dark wings **marabou storks** look like mournful undertakers...58 - Primeval in appearance, **giant lizards** look disturbingly like dragons...60 - With their slender bodies and beautiful mottled coats, **giraffes** are the supermodels of the savanna...62 - Reputedly bad tempered, in reality **water buffaloes** are extremely gentle giants...66 - Fascinating and elusive, **giant squid** have the largest eyes in the animal kingdom...68 - With their power, strength and aerobatic skills, **bald eagles** are real high fliers...70 - In spite of their corpulent bodies, **crocodiles** are not big eaters...72 - Ivory tusks make **walruses** the 'elephants' of the Arctic...76 - Slow-moving and clumsy on land, **hippopotamuses** are extremely agile in water...78 - In spite of their good-natured appearance, **Kodiak bears** are fierce animals who live by their strength...80

Relentlessly hunted for their ivory tusks, elephants are now an endangered species

THE WORLD'S LARGEST MAMMALS ARE DEFENCELESS AGAINST IVORY POACHERS

The majestic elephant of the African savanna is the most impressive of the world's large mammals. The males stand 4 metres high at the shoulder and weigh 6 tonnes! The largest recorded specimen, killed in Angola, weighed over 10 tonnes. The elephant's trade marks are its long trunk, big ears and tusks. The longest elephant tusks – the right tusk measures 3.49 metres – were found in the Democratic Republic of the Congo (formerly Zaïre). Today, they form part of Geological Society of America's collection of skulls and horns in New York. The heaviest pair of tusks (211 kilograms) can be seen in the British Museum in London. Tusks have long been the object of a flourishing trade that began in Africa in the 19th century. By the end of the 1980s, some 90,000 elephants were being killed each year. Public opinion, incensed by this mass slaughter, demanded that the ivory trade be outlawed.

Profile

African elephant
Loxodonta africana
Family: Elephantidae
Size: 3 m to 4 m at the shoulder
Weight: 4 tonnes to 6 tonnes (males); 3 tonnes to 4 tonnes (females)
Habitat: all types of environment except desert
Diet: strict herbivore (depending on the season, an individual's daily intake varies between 150 kg and 280 kg of grass, leaves, bushes and fruit)
Gestation period: 22 months
Number of young: 1 (approx. 120 kg at birth)
Life expectancy: 50 to 60 years
Number: 600,000

Elephants help to maintain the ecological balance of the African savanna. By eating plants that would otherwise become too invasive, they create an environment that favours the greatest number of animal species.

Elephants live in herds, organized around a few females (matriarchs) and their offspring. They form a close-knit family unit and often seek auditory, visual and tactile contact in which the trunk plays a major role. Elephants use their tusks (the equivalent of incisors) when feeding, and to defend themselves when attacked.

The Asian elephant uses its trunk for a number of purposes, including taking a dust shower.

Asian elephants

Asian elephants (*Elephas maximus*) live in the tropical forests of Asia. The females and young form small communities, while the males are often solitary. There are an estimated 30,000 to 40,000 Asian elephants scattered, in small populations, throughout Nepal, Burma, southern China, Laos, Thailand, Malaysia, Sumatra in northern Borneo (where they are thought to have returned to the wild after being introduced by humans), Kerala (south-west India), Assam (north-east India) and Sri Lanka. They live to about the age of 70.

SMALLER ASIAN COUSINS

Unlike the African civilizations, whose relationship with elephants has often been confrontational, Asian elephants are highly venerated. The Hindu god of knowledge and prophecy is the elephant-headed god Ganesa. Asian elephants have also been domesticated for a very long time, especially in India. They have a more rounded body and are smaller than their African cousins, rarely exceeding 3 metres in height or 3 tonnes in weight. Their ears are smaller and their tusks straighter and shorter, sometimes barely even noticeable. The females and 40 percent of males have no tusks at all.

Although the widespread slaughter of the elephant population extended into Asia, this part of the world has deified the elephant. It has also harnessed the elephants' strength and docility, especially in the forests of India where they may haul up to 2 tonnes of timber and carry loads of between 500 and 600 kilograms. Once used to their mahout (elephant driver), they serve him faithfully.

Elephants are born after 22 months' gestation. These impressive babies weigh between 115 and 120 kilograms and are able to walk immediately. They gain between 9 and 20 kilograms a month until the age of four. Elephants appear to keep growing throughout their life and the weight of adults of the same age varies considerably.

African elephants are extremely dependent on water and consume 80 litres a day. During the dry seas hundreds of kilometres in search of a waterhole or swamp. When they get there, they take preced quenching their thirst, they take mudbaths to rid themselves of parasites which are crushed by t'

The largest dolphins, orcs are the scourge of the seas

The sound of an orc's tail hitting the water can be heard several kilometres away.

Orcs always 'patrol' in groups of between 5 and 20. Although adult males – recognizable by their long dorsal fin – may occasionally move away from the group in search of food, they always remain within hearing distance.

KILLERS IN DINNER JACKETS

Orcs (*Orcinus orca*), also known as killer whales, are the largest members of the dolphin family (Delphinidae). They can grow to a length of 9.5 metres, while their large, erect dorsal fin can measure up to two metres. The males weigh in at 8 tonnes, while the females are much lighter at around 4 tonnes. Their characteristic black and white markings provide excellent camouflage by breaking up their outline and enabling them to swim unseen through the grey waters in pursuit of prey. These discreet but deadly hunters are also remarkably agile. They patrol the shores of the world's oceans, but prefer colder waters. They are voracious carnivores and their readiness to attack sea lions, whales and even other members of the dolphin family has earned them the name 'killer whale'.

An orc's impressive mouth contains about 50 teeth, each around 12 to 14 centimetres long, which slot neatly together. Its powerful jaws enable this relentless hunter to grip and devour extremely large prey (whales) as well as smaller marine mammals (sea lions, seals).

The orc has three characteristic white markings on its back and underside: the roughly moon-shaped area, rather like a saddle, behind the dorsal fin; the elongated area on its head, just above the eye; the trident-shaped area (the largest of the three) covering the whole of the underside.

With their gliding flight
condors
are the lords of the air

Condors consume 900 grams of food a day, but they can eat much more than this and also tolerate prolonged periods of fasting.

A MAJESTIC GLIDER

With a wingspan of over 3 metres, the Andean condor (*Vultur gryphus*) – found in the Andes mountains of South America – is one of the world's largest and most impressive birds. The width of its wings is as important as their length in determining the aerofoil (the surface that produces lift and controls flight). A large surface is vital given that these great birds can weigh up to 11 kilograms. However, such a wingspan is not without its disadvantages, especially when taking off. This does not present a problem if the condor launches itself into the air from a cliff, but it has to run to take off from the ground. Once airborne, this huge bird of prey adopts a majestic gliding flight, describing huge sweeping circles as it searches for carrion.

The condor's beak attests to its carnivorous lifestyle. Hooked and razor-sharp, it is ideal for tearing at carrion, while its bald head and neck are well suited to rummaging around inside carcasses. The distinctive crest is an exclusively male attribute.

The mating display of the Andean condor is in fact quite discreet. The male stands near the female and opens and closes his wings alternately. He then 'bows', pointing his head downwards and clicking his tongue rapidly against his beak, before turning his back on the female. This is an invitation for her to indicate her consent by caressing her partner's head and beak with her own.

The large feathers on the wing tips act as independent aerofoils.

Profile

Andean condor
Vultur gryphus
Family: Cathartidae

Wingspan: 2.9 m to 3.2 m
Weight: 11 kg to 12 kg (males); 7.5 kg to 10 kg (females)
Habitat: mainly mountainous regions; western coasts of South America
Diet: mainly carrion; some live prey
Incubation period: 54 to 58 days
Number of eggs per brood: 1 or 2; the chicks weigh 180 g when they hatch
Life expectancy: up to 60 years in captivity

CONSCIENTIOUS PARENTS

For most of the year, condors live in groups. In July and August, they pair off and begin to look for a secluded nest site, usually on an inaccessible rocky ledge. Once they have chosen a site, the female lays her large, white egg(s) – each weighing the equivalent of four chicken's eggs (280 grams) – directly on to the rock. The male and female take it in turns to incubate the egg(s), sitting for up to 20 hours at a stretch (with a record of 46 hours) without food. These huge birds of prey are able to tolerate prolonged periods of fasting.

After two months, a fragile featherless chick hatches from the egg. Condors are conscientious parents and keep the chick warm day and night. They continue to feed it until it is able to fend for itself. Young condors begin to learn to fly from the age of 5 months, but do not fully master the art until they are between 10 and 12 months old.

A partisan of 'minimum effort'

Bearing in mind its weight and size, the condor would have to have extremely impressive pectoral muscles if it had to flap its wings to take off and to remain airborne. Instead, it uses the large aerofoil of its great wings to glide upwards on the warm air currents. This means that the condor has to wait for the sun to warm up the land before it can take to the skies. Then, with the minimum of effort, this great bird of prey is able to soar high in the sky, wheeling and circling for hours at a time without becoming tired.

The Andes are the natural habitat of the great condor, which rests in groups or nests in pairs on their steep slopes and sheer cliffs. It is impossible to imagine the Andes without the condor.

With their magnificent antlers, red deer are the aristocrats of the forest

During the rutting season, the males do not tolerate rivals. If their body language does not dissuade other aspiring suitors, combat is the only alternative. Although rare, these combats always follow the same pattern. The two adversaries run at each other, at full tilt, and their antlers clash noisily. Often, one of the combatants retreats after the initial exchanges.

A ROYAL CROWN

The red deer (*Cervus elaphus*), the aristocrat of the Cervidae family, is a large mammal, which stands up to 1.5 metres at the shoulder, measures between 1.7 and 2.2 metres in length and weighs over 200 kilograms. It is the deer's antlers that give it such an aristocratic air. The red deer of Eastern Europe have larger, heavier (15 kilograms) antlers than their western European cousins, whose antlers weigh a maximum of 5 kilograms. Their North American counterparts, known as wapitis or American elk (*Cervus elaphus canadensis*), are even bigger (weighing around 400 kilograms) and their antlers can reach a length of 1.5 metres and weigh up to 25 kilograms.

During the mating (rutting) season, rivalry between evenly matched males is common, although it doesn't necessarily end in combat. The rivals size each other up and try to assert their dominance by belling (bellowing) and using body language to issue a warning. This often involves walking parallel to their rival, showing off their shoulder muscles, displaying their antlers, grinding their teeth and rolling their eyes.

The red deer, originally a native of Asia, is today mainly found in the forests of the northern hemisphere. It has also been introduced into countries in the southern hemisphere: Argentina, Chile, New Zealand. These animals are constantly on the move and require extensive territories. A family of three moves within an area of between 500 and 1500 hectares, while an adult male covers 2000 to 5000 hectares.

Known as the red deer in Europe and the wapiti or American elk in North America, this aristocrat of the Cervidae family has adapted admirably to temperature variations in the northern – and even the southern – hemisphere.

Profile

Red deer
Cervus elaphus
Family: Cervidae
Size: 1.6 m at the shoulder
Weight: 100 kg (Scotland) to 450 kg (North American male)
Habitat: great broadleaved and coniferous forests, grasslands and prairies (Scotland, United States, Asia)
Diet: herbivore
Gestation period: 34 weeks
Life expectancy: 14 to 15 years, maximum of 25 years in captivity

Belling

The term 'belling' refers to the bellowing cry of the males during the rutting (mating) season. Male deer, silent during the rest of the year, begin to bell at the end of August in the areas frequented by the hinds (females). Dominant stags gather herds of females together and guard them jealously. During the rutting season, these usually sociable animals will not tolerate the presence of a potential rival and use belling to assert their dominance and issue a warning. Although belling usually avoids the need for combat, the hierarchy is sometimes challenged by a physical confrontation. From dawn to dusk, the forest resounds to the awesome 'belling' of rutting deer. The huge males extend their necks and raise their heads to utter this prolonged and raucous cry. At the height of the rutting season, the males bell day and night.

MALE 'HEADGEAR'

All ruminants have some form of 'frontal appendage': cattle have horns, and deer have antlers. Antlers are solid, bony projections attached to two protruberences on the front of the skull. This characteristically male 'headgear' starts to appear when the young deer are nine or ten months old, and begins to branch into tines when they are in their second year. Male deer shed their antlers every year at the end of winter. The antlers are replaced almost immediately by new ones.

The length and size of the antlers is more important than the number of tines. Deer tend to live in social groups (herds), with the females living separately for most of the year, and a male's antlers are an indication of his social status. They also indicate his dominance and act as a deterrent during the rutting season. However, the shedding process has the effect of temporarily reversing the established order since the older males shed their antlers first. The young males take their revenge by obliging their elders to take the lead if the herd is forced into flight.

The deer has always been associated with legend and mythology. In Europe, deer appear in the 17,000-year-old cave paintings of Lascaux in the Dordogne (France), where they are thought to illustrate a ritual designed to bring hunters good luck. In Asian mythology, the deer led the dead into the afterlife, while Native Americans art often depicted a tree growing from a deer's antlers.

Today **bison** are the heaviest mammals in Europe

The European bison population has increased to three million.

The bison's hairy head, low head carriage and dark, smouldering eyes suggest fierce determination and power. This huge yet agile mammal has little to fear, except perhaps, the guns of the would-be 'Buffalo Bills' who, in just a few years in the 19th century, almost exterminated this magnificent creature.

SURVIVORS OF THE 'OLD WORLD'

In the 8th and 9th centuries, the European bison population (*Bison bonasus*) extended across Europe to the borders of Switzerland and, by the mid-18th century, had spread to the Asian part of Russia. Today, the only wild bison in Europe live in the forests of Bialowieski Park in Poland, where the population was re-established in 1956 using a few pure-bred animals raised in captivity. Today, the bison is Europe's largest mammal and can stand 2 metres at the shoulder and weigh almost a tonne. Males reach maturity at the age of eight and females at the age of five. In spite of its great weight, it shows great speed and agility. It can achieve speeds of up to 50 kilometres an hour and is able to clear obstacles, jumping horizontal distances of up to 3 metres!

Forests are the bison's natural habitat. In spring, European bison favour the cool broadleaved forests with their dense undergrowth, streams, marshes and clearings, although they are also found in mixed forests. They spend one third of their time eating (consuming 25 kilograms of vegetation every day) and the other two thirds resting and ruminating.

...AND THEIR 'NEW-WORLD' COUSINS

Today, American bison (*Bison bison*) live on game reserves. With their characteristically massive head and shoulders and disproportionately slender hindquarters, they are smaller and stockier than their European cousins. Males can reach a height of 1.8 metres at the shoulder and weigh up to 1.35 tonnes. They have a large, woolly head with bright black, heavy-lidded eyes and black horns that curve upwards and inwards. Their coat consists of long, coarse hair and a woolly 'fleece' that is replaced twice a year. Their rather short legs end in large, rounded hooves.

AN INDIAN FETISH

In the mid-16th century, a Spanish conquistador reported that there were so many American bison, it was impossible to count them. In fact, their vast numbers (around 60 million) represented the world's highest ever concentration of large mammals. By the end of the 19th century, only a few hundred remained. They had been systematically exterminated by white settlers in an attempt to subjugate the Native Americans. Native Americans believed that the Great Spirit had created the bison to provide food and clothing for the first human beings to inhabit the Earth. However, the Spirit had also warned that when the bison disappeared from Earth, the end of humanity was nigh.

Fighting by the rules

During the mating season, bison engage in violent combats, accompanied by much bellowing, pawing of the ground and snorting. They lower their head and charge, fighting head to head or using their head to strike their opponent. They use all the strength of their great muscular neck and forequarters to push their opponent backwards, but they also observe certain rules. They don't attack from the side, as this would be dangerous, and they always wait for their adversary to be squarely positioned before resuming the fight.

The Native Americans used the tanned hide of the bison to make clothing, moccasins and teepees, while the thick hide of the neck was used for warriors' shields. The sinews made excellent bowstrings, the stomach was made into a water skin and the meat fed the entire tribe. A bison provided the Native Americans with 125 different items and raw materials and they never killed more than they needed.

Like slow-moving tanks on legs, giant tortoises seem to have emerged from the depths of time

The giant tortoises of the Galápagos Islands move slowly and silently, one behind the other, along the same paths which are like roads cut through the undergrowth. Their slow pace and longevity are legendary. Most of the tortoises born on these Pacific islands live for 100 years. Along with the giant tortoises of the Seychelles, they are the world's largest terrestrial tortoises.

2000 TIMES THEIR ORIGINAL WEIGHT

The female Galápagos tortoise digs in the ground for several hours with her hind legs before laying her clutch of between two and eight round, white eggs. The eggs incubate for eight to twelve weeks, although the incubation period can extend to eight months if the climatic conditions are not right. The newly born tortoises are minute and usually weigh about 90 grams. They are abandoned by the adults who leave them to fend for themselves and find their own way to the high ground inhabited by the other tortoises. The adults often weigh over 200 kilograms and keep growing, at a fairly rapid rate, throughout their extremely long lives.

The tortoise only has its long neck to enable it to reach fruit that has fallen to the ground or tall plants that take its fancy. It holds the plant with its tongue and cuts it off with the finely serrated edges of its jaws. It takes the tortoise a long time to chew large pieces of vegetation, which it chops down by moving its jaws to and fro and crushing them with its tongue.

Although toothless, the jaws of the tortoise are razor sharp.

A CUMBERSOME CARAPACE

The distinguishing feature of a tortoise is the carapace or shell that protects its entire body. When frightened, a Galápagos tortoise pulls in its neck, which folds up rather like a concertina, and draws its head and legs into its shell. The shell also acts as a food store that the tortoise can draw on when the vegetation is poor, and provides protection against major variations in temperature.

The shell is divided into three parts: the upper shell (carapace) which is high domed and raised above the neck area; the lower shell (plastron) which is flat in the female and concave in the male to make mating easier; and the 'bridge' that links the carapace and plastron on either side of the animal's body. Covering – and attached to – the bony inner layer are scale-like keratin plates (shields), rounded at the corners, that can become detached individually. The heavy shell of the Seychelles tortoise is dark grey and very high domed.

Profile

Giant Galápagos tortoise
Chelonoidis elephantopus
Size: up to 122 cm
Weight: over 200 kg
Habitat: slopes of the Cerro Azul volcano (Galápagos Islands in the South Pacific)
Life expectancy: about 100 years

Giant Seychelles tortoise
Dipsochelys elephantina
Size: up to 130 cm
Habitat: grassy areas and mangroves of the Aldabra Islands (south-west of the Seychelles, in the Indian Ocean)
Life expectancy: record of 152 years

A long and extremely useful neck

The movements of the Galápagos tortoise are hampered by its hard shell. However, it has a very long neck covered with thick, supple skin which allows it to move in all directions. This is very useful for ridding itself of the ticks and parasites that inhabit the folds of its skin, or for reaching the plants on which its feeds. It is also used to store water as the tortoise has to drink a great deal. When it finds water, it drinks as much as possible, sucking it in through its barely open, toothless jaws, and storing upto several litres in its neck.

Although the Galápagos tortoise doesn't mind being used as a perch by an eagle, it prefers the finches that rid it of its parasites.

Their graceful leaps belie the fact that
whales
weigh as much as a herd of elephants

Whales can remain submerged for more than 20 minutes. A blowhole, a sort of nostril closed by a double valve when it dives, enables a whale to breathe on the surface and not breathe under water. When it resurfaces, the jet of air emitted through this blowhole can be seen over a great distance. The jet emitted by the blue whale can reach a height of 15 metres, while that of the humpback whale is more modest at only 3 metres.

GIANTS OF THE SEA

The humpback whale (*Megaptera novaeangliae*), with its characteristic tail fin, is aptly named in Latin: megaptera comes from the Greek megas meaning 'huge, powerful' and pteron meaning 'wing'. Although only 19 metres long, the humpback weighs 48 tonnes. However, it is not as impressive as the blue whale (*Sibbaldus* – or *Balaenoptera* – *musculus*) of which the largest specimen on record, a female captured in 1909, measured 33 metres. On March 20, 1947, a Soviet whaler brought a 190-tonne female back from the Antarctic – the equivalent of 37 elephants! Its tongue weighed 4.29 tonnes and its heart 698.5 kilograms.

The humpback whale is a superb diver and can reach depths of 250 metres. Its body is about 20 metres long and its tail is between 2 and 3 metres wide. The tail consists of two horizontal fins with no bony supports. Its strength and suppleness comes from a network of tendons and fibres.

A net of bubbles

After locating a shoal of plankton or krill, the whale dives beneath it and then rises slowly to the surface. As it does so, it releases air and thousands of tiny air bubbles form a fine net that ensnares the tiny shrimp-like creatures. The whale opens its mouth wide and swallows a mouthful of several tonnes.

Terrifying legends

Unlike the dolphin, the whale has always inspired fear in humans and been regarded as an enemy. The Bible tells how Jonah was swallowed by a whale and spent three days and nights in its stomach before being regurgitated into the sea. The Roman writer and naturalist, Gaius Plinius Secundus, better known as Pliny the Elder (23–79 AD), described a huge fish called a physeter ('blower' in Greek) that emerged from the sea like a column or pillar, taller than the sails of any ship, and sent vast quantities of water high into the air as if emitting it from a pipe. Scandinavian and Icelandic texts from the Middle Ages are full of stories about whales, which are always surrounded by mystery and fear. Whales were not observed scientifically until the 18th century and, in 1758, cetaceans (whales, dolphins, porpoises, rorquals) were definitively classified as mammals and not fish. Sadly, people only began to take a real interest in these huge creatures, which they had mercilessly hunted for their meat and oil, when they had virtually wiped them out.

This spectacular leap by a humpback whale shows its two long pectoral fins, the equivalent of the front legs of land mammals. The significance of these leaps is still unknown: they could be a type of game, a means of communication, a display of strength or a mating ritual.

23

A humpback whale may have up to 500 kilograms of acorn barnacles attached to its skin.

A huge appetite

Hungry after their six-month winter fast, humpback whales leave the warm waters of the tropics for the colder, food-rich waters of the polar regions. In spring, under the combined effect of rising water temperatures and longer daylight hours, the supply of plankton in these polar waters increases. The fish, shrimps and krill (small, shrimp-like crustaceans that live in huge shoals) that feed on the plankton are in turn eaten by whales. And whales are capable of eating a huge quantity of fish! Their stomachs can hold 600 herrings or sardines and 700 kilograms of cod and plankton…

ENDANGERED SPECIES

The threat of extinction due to over-fishing led the International Whaling Commission (IWC), in 1937, to impose restrictions on hunting humpback whales in the Antarctic. Humpbacks subsequently became a protected species in the Antarctic (1956), southern hemisphere (1963) and North Pacific (1966). In 1982, the IWC introduced an eight-year international ban on commercial whaling. In spite of this, species such as the Arctic (or bowhead) whale (*Balaena mysticetus*) are still threatened with extinction.

Baby whales are born underwater in warm tropical waters where they can maintain their body temperature without using up too many calories, and build up their strength for the long journey to the cold polar waters. They do not leave their mother's side, sometimes even riding on her back, and do not become really independent until the age of four. Humpback whales live for up to 30 years.

A common rorqual (*Balaenoptera physalus*) swims through a shoal of plankton and krill with its mouth wide open, swallowing several tonnes of water. It empties the water from its mouth through the strips of whalebone located between its jaws. This strains the plankton and krill from the water.

Is this manoeuvre designed to intimidate a rival or seduce a female? In one incredible movement, the males project their 48-tonne bodies almost vertically out of the water. When only their tail remains submerged, these huge acrobats execute an about-turn so that they fall backwards on to the water, hitting the surface with a thunderous crash.

Lords of the Arctic, polar bears are the world's largest carnivores

The polar bear's white fur provides excellent camouflage for hunting seals on the ice floes.

A SEAL AT EVERY MEAL

Polar bears – with grizzly bears and the Kodiak bears of Alaska – are the world's largest carnivores. The males can reach up to 2.5 metres in length and weigh 410 kilograms. These lords of the Arctic are solitary creatures and ideally suited to life in the icy polar waters. They are skilled hunters, with seals accounting for 90 percent of their diet. They rarely catch seals in the water, but usually take them by surprise on an ice floe or when they come up for air in an ice hole. The bears wait patiently for the end of a snout to appear and deal the unsuspecting seal a formidable blow with one of their huge paws.

Hungry as a lion

Polar bears are incredibly strong and can lift animals weighing up to 100 kilograms with a single paw. Although usually slow-moving animals, they can reach speeds of between 30 and 40 kilometres an hour when pursuing their prey. But in spite of their great hunting skills, they often return empty handed. In fact they are only successful in 18 percent of cases. To maintain their body weight, polar bears must kill a seal every five to six days. However, if the need arises, they can fast for several weeks as their stomach can hold almost 70 kilograms of food.

The cubs experience their first outing when the family leaves its winter quarters. They keep close to their mother and will stay with her for the next year or two.

The polar bear's scientific name *Ursus maritimus*, 'sea bear', is apt: this white bear is a very accomplished swimmer and diver.

These playful young bears are in fact developing their reflexes.

YOUNG AT HEART

Polar bears love to play, especially when they are young. But their games also serve to prepare them for their life as hunters. As they mature, they still like to play. One of their favourite games is to stand on their hind legs and 'embrace' their opponent with their front paws, each taking great care not to hurt the other. After this heavy, lumbering 'bear hug', the contestants sink to the ground exhausted.

Profile

Polar bear
Ursus maritimus
Family: Ursidae

Size: 2 m to 2.5 m (males); 1.8 m to 2.1 m (females)
Weight: 410 kg (males); 320 kg (females)
Habitat: frozen shores and ice floes on the edge of the Arctic ice field
Diet: carnivore (seals)
Gestation period: 7 to 9 months
Number of young: usually 2, exceptionally 1 or 3
Life expectancy: 25 years; record of 34 years

It is a well-known fact that pregnant females hibernate in the den where they give birth. However, recent research has shown that males and young bears are not active all year round either, even though they do not hibernate as such. It is thought that they can 'hibernate' as they move around and are able to pass from a lethargic to an active state at will.

They may not be able to fly, but ostriches are fast on their feet

Rhea's egg usually measure 12.5 by 8.5 centimetres and weigh 550 grammes.

The Australian cassowary has a characteristic bony crest and powerful, three-toed feet. This a squat bird with its average-length neck is the world's second largest bird after the ostrich. The cassowary is a fruit-eating bird.

THE WORLD'S LARGEST EGGS

The ostrich is the largest and tallest of the large, flightless birds: rheas, emus, cassowaries, kiwis. The males can reach a height of 2.75 metres and weigh up to 150 kilos. These giant proportions are reflected in its eggs which, on average, measure 16 by 13 centimetres and weigh between 750 and 1600 grammes. They can represent the equivalent of 30 chicken's eggs.

Although the ostrich cannot fly, its long legs and powerful thighs enable it to run extremely fast. It is the only bird in the world to have two-toed feet, while its impressive leg muscles enable it to run at speeds of between 30 and 50 kilometres an hour for fifteen or even thirty minutes. If pressed, it can reach 70 kilometres an hour.

The three-toed emu is a native of Australia. Its has brownish plumage, which also covers its neck and thighs, and a blackish head with areas of blue skin on either side. The male incubates the eggs laid by several females. Emus are unpopular with stock farmers, who consider they feed at the expense of their cattle and sheep, and have been the subject of widespread extermination programmes.

Ostriches have the feathers of a cabaret star and the legs of an athlete. They only use their wings with their huge feathers for displays, to keep themselves cool or to protect their young. During mating displays, the males spread their wings to make themselves look more imposing and to impress their rivals.

In South Africa, ostriches are farmed in semi-liberty for their feathers, eggs and skin. These farms also organise ostrich races in which each bird has its own `jockey'. The birds' great size and muscular frame make them easy to ride.

With their fearsome fangs and claws, **tigers** are terrifying and fascinating creatures

Tigers mark out their territory with strategically located faeces or by spraying urine mixed with strong-smelling secretions from their anal glands. These 'markers' act as a repellent and warning to other tigers. They are reinforced by visual warnings such as claw marks on tree trunks.

SUDDEN, VIOLENT ATTACKS

In the still night air, a tiger is stalking its prey, moving slowly and silently on its velvet paws. Its tawny yellow coat marked with black stripes provides perfect camouflage amongst the tall grasses, while thickets are the ideal place for an ambush. Crouching low, its tail erect and ears flat against its head, this giant feline tenses its muscles and leaps forward like an uncoiled spring. The attack is sudden and violent and, a few seconds later, the tiger gives a mighty roar as its victim lies between its huge front paws. Unless they are starving, tigers carry their prey to a more secluded spot where they can enjoy their meal undisturbed.

The mating season is the only time tigers associate with other tigers. The female comes into heat for about a week every one to three months. Some couples remain together for over a week. In the event that several – extremely jealous – males are attracted to the same tigress, confrontation is inevitable.

When a tiger spots its prey, it lies in wait, motionless. If it does move, it advances slowly, a step at a time, but usually waits for its victim to move to within a dozen or so metres of where it is lying. Then the tiger launches an attack – with a leap of up to 6 metres – that is determined by the type of terrain and position of its prey. However, in spite of its great energy, these attacks are often unsuccessful.

Profile

Tiger
Panthera tigris
Family: Felidae
Size: 1.4 m to 1.8 m without the tail (60 cm to 95 cm)
Weight: 180 kg to 250 kg (male); 100 kg to 160 kg (female)
Habitat: Asia, from the tropical jungle to the Siberian taiga
Diet: carnivore
Gestation period: 98 to 110 days
Number of young: usually 2; maximum 5 in the wild (7 in captivity)
Life expectancy: 26 years
Number: 4000 to 7000

THE LARGEST OF THE BIG CATS

The Siberian tiger (*Panthera tigris altaica*) is a giant among tigers and the largest of the big cats. The largest tiger on record was a Siberian tiger which measured 2.8 metres in length and weighed 384 kilograms. These solitary animals inhabit vast territories in the mixed (coniferous and oak) forests of the northern hemisphere. Meetings between males and females are few and far between. However, in spite of the harsh conditions threatening their survival in the wild, they are not an endangered species. There are more Siberian tigers in captivity than in the wild, and most of the 1000 tigers in captivity are in fact Siberian tigers.

White tigers are in fact a type of Indian tiger. Their cream coat is the result of a mutation of the gene responsible for colour. A 'white tiger' is produced when both parents carry the mutated gene. In 1951, the Maharajah of Rewa was so fascinated by their strange beauty that he established a breeding programme for these beautiful creatures that are rarely found in the wild.

Of the seven other subspecies, the Indian tiger (*Panthera tigris tigris*), is most common in the wild: 5000 individuals (4000 of them in India). The others are the Indochinese tiger (*Panthera tigris corbetti*), Chinese tiger (*Panthera tigris amoyensis*), Caspian tiger (*Panthera tigris virgata*), which became extinct in the mid-20th century, Sumatran tiger (*Panthera tigris sumatrae*) and extinct Javan (*Panthera tigris sondaica*) and Balinese (*Panthera tigris balica*) tigers.

Man-eaters?

The tiger is among the animals responsible for the greatest number of human deaths as a result of direct attack. In the 19th century, a single tiger is reported to have killed some 430 people in India. It is in fact the loss of its natural habitat due to increased human activity that has led to the tiger's abnormal behaviour, and this is reflected in the increasing number of confrontations with humans. Tigers may also attack humans when suffering from wounds that have left them unable to hunt their normal prey.

Distribution

Tigers used to be found throughout most of Asia. Over the last 100 years, they have been confined to increasingly restricted areas and are now found in only a few places concentrated along the Tropic of Cancer. The Siberian tiger is found only in the densely wooded areas of Asia and feeds on a wide variety of different animals that it hunts by stalking.

Tigers are extremely playful creatures, especially when young. They are also excellent swimmers and love water. They are particularly fond of streams and rivers since, when they are not in the water, the grasses and bushes on the banks offer a cool place to rest during the hottest hours of the day.

Siren or sea cow, **manatees** are gentle, harmless creatures

It may look like a sea monster, but the manatee is completely harmless. They are hunted by few predators: sharks, crocodiles, alligators and humans.

A SLOW-MOVING, GENEROUSLY PROPORTIONED SIREN

Female manatees are larger than the males and reach up to 4.5 metres in length. The record weight for a manatee is a tonne. Although identified as sirens by the early navigators, they have little in common with the sea nymphs of mythology who lured sailors onto the rocks with their singing. Also known as 'sea cows', these slow-moving 'chilly' mammals live peaceably in the warm waters off the coast of America and in African river estuaries. Unlike other cetaceans (dolphins, porpoises, rorquals), they are not fast-moving streamlined swimmers. Added to this, their extremely trusting nature means they are easily hunted down by crocodiles, sharks and, more scandalously, humans.

Today, most of the manatees killed off the coast of Florida are the victims of collisions with speed boats. This manatee (right) cannot swim properly as its broad, flattened tail, which acts as a sort of rudder, has been damaged by a propeller.

The manatee's massive, oval body is flattened on the back and covered with sparse hair on the underside. It has a rounded head with no external ear parts, tiny eyes and a whiskered snout. Its high-placed nostrils enable it to breathe unseen before diving back below the surface. Although charming, the manatee is a far cry from the sirens described in Homer's *Odyssey*.

The distribution of manatees is linked to water temperature and the availablity of food. They tend to be found in freshwater estuaries rather than salt water.

The elongated position of the manatee's lungs enable it to swim horizontally and even control its water line between the river bed and the surface. Its main means of propulsion is its broad, spatula-shaped tail. It swims at between 3 and 7 kilometres an hour, but if it is being hunted or simply in a hurry, it can reach speeds of up to 25 kilometres an hour.

Renowned for swallowing their victims whole, giant snakes have always been the object of great fascination

Today, the world's largest snakes are found in the constrictor family (Boidae). While boa constrictors rarely exceed 3 metres in length, anacondas and certain pythons (such as the reticulate python) can be as much as 8 metres long.

ANACONDAS AND PYTHONS: THE WORLD'S LARGEST AND LONGEST SNAKES

The giant anaconda (*Eunetes murinus*), a relative of the famous boa constrictor, is found in the tropical regions of America. With a length of between 8 and 9 metres, it is certainly an alarming proposition and the longest American snake. Although the reticulate python (*Python reticulatus*) can match it in terms of length (some even exceed 10 metres), the anaconda is larger and heavier and can weigh up to 200 kilograms. A specimen observed in the delta of the Orinoco River (Venezuela) measured 90 centimetres in diameter! The anaconda is also the most aquatic of the giant snakes, even though it feeds on land animals that come to drink on the banks and shores of rivers and lakes.

All snakes are carnivorous. Constrictors – boas, anacondas and pythons – hold their prey with their jaws and suffocate it in the powerful and deadly embrace of their coils. They then begin to swallow their victim head first. Above we see an anaconda coiled around a common iguana.

Profile

Anaconda
Eunetes murinus
Size: up to 9 m
Weight: up to 180 kg
Habitat: dense tropical forests on the edge of rivers, lakes and pools, east of the Andes and in southern Paraguay

COLOSSAL STRENGTH, MODEST APPETITE

Anacondas and reticulate pythons capture their prey by striking suddenly and unexpectedly. Like all constrictors, they actually kill their victim by suffocation. One reticulate python, measuring 5 metres in length and weighing 31 kilograms, was seen devouring a pig of around 9 kilograms.

Because they swallow their prey whole, it can take these giant snakes up to an hour to actually ingest such a large meal, while the next few days are spent digesting it. This is in fact a relatively short time considering the size of their prey. Although able to swallow huge amounts at a time, on average, these great reptiles only eat just over their own body weight in a year. They can also fast for a whole year at a time!

Profile

Reticulate python
Python reticulatus
Size: over 10 m
Habitat: rainforests, woodlands and meadows of South-east Asia (Indochina), slow-moving rivers near the Pacific coast (Philippines and Sunda Islands).

When relaxing, these giant snakes 'curl up' with their head resting in the centre of the coils formed by their body.
Each species (reticulate python, above) has its own distinctive geometrically patterned skin and different coloured scales.
Snakes renew their remarkably supple skin on a regular basis by shedding the outer layer. The discarded skin is known as the 'slough'.

In spite of their great size, gorillas are shy and retiring creatures

Mountain gorillas live in the Virunga Mountains on the borders of the Congo (formerly Zaïre), Rwanda and Uganda.

FROM TINY BABY TO GENTLE GIANT

Along with the chimpanzee, the gorilla – the largest and strongest member of the monkey family – is the animal that most resembles human beings. Strangely enough, a baby gorilla is only half the weight (1.5 kilograms) of a human baby at birth, while adults grow to a height of between 1.4 and 2 metres and weigh between 140 and 200 kilograms (males), or 70 to 110 kilograms (females). This huge primate has a low forehead and very prominent eyebrow arches. Its arms are longer than its legs and, like its legs, are muscular and powerful. These anthropoids ('resembling man') are divided into three subspecies or races: the western lowland gorilla, the eastern lowland gorilla and the mountain gorilla.

The only enemies of these peaceable forest-dwellers are humans, and if humans try to kill them or steal their young, then gorillas are extremely dangerous animals. These usually non-aggressive vegetarians know how to defend themselves and will fight to the last.

Babies are spoiled by all members of the gorilla community. They have little in the way of innate behaviour and their progress during the early months of their life is governed by their mother and other members of the group. During their early development, the older gorillas play with the babies, tickle them, cuddle them and turn a blind eye to their silly pranks. Gorillas live, on average, for thirty years.

By the time male gorillas become sexually mature at around 15 years old, the black hair on their lower backs has been replaced by a broad band of greyish-white hair. These males are referred to as 'silver backs'. The skin on the face, ears, palms of the hand, soles of the feet and upper part of the chest is black and hairless. The dominant male in each family group is usually the oldest 'silver back'.

Young males often act as 'sentries'. The importance of respecting personal space is a lesson learnt early in a gorilla's life.
When resting during the day and settling down for the night, each member of the group constructs its own nest, usually on the ground. Gorillas tend to avoid 'nesting' in trees due to their lack of agility and great weight.

The world's largest anthropoid ape gives voice to his superior might. In spite of their impressive appearance, these hairy, muscular giants are in fact non-aggressive and entirely vegetarian. However, male gorillas will fight to the death to defend the members of their family group. In this patriarchal society, females are often the object of bloody conflicts between males.

On their huge wings, albatrosses glide high above the cold southern oceans

Immediately after hatching, the young albatross is extremely vulnerable. However, with its insistent demands for food, it soon grows to almost the size of its parents although its beak is not as strong. At eight months, it still has traces of its pale down, but by a year old, it has characteristic brown plumage. The young albatross makes its maiden flight about nine months after hatching.

AN IMPRESSIVE WINGSPAN

The albatross is particularly noted for its great wingspan which can be as much as 3.5 metres. In spite of its size – about 2.5 metres – this magnificent seabird only weighs about 10 kilograms. Its great hooked beak, up to 18 centimetres long, is extremely useful for fishing but also makes a formidable weapon in the event of a dispute. The albatross not only consumes large amounts of fish, but also cuttlefish, squid and shrimps which it catches with great skill and precision by gliding above the water and skimming the surface with its beak. Since it would require considerable energy to flap its great wings, the albatross usually adopts a gliding flight using the wind and air currents.

During its mating display, the wandering albatross (*Diomedea exulans*) adopts a position of greeting known as 'presentation'. It stands firmly on its big webbed feet, spreads its wings, raises its head and utters piercing cries. Once the display is over, the two birds settle down side by side and preen each others feathers.

Albatrosses spend most of their long life (up to 35 years) gliding high above the cold oceans of the southern hemisphere. However, they do take the occasional break and touch down to nest, for example. They remain faithful throughout their lives and the same male and female always build their nest together, even if they have been separated during the past year.

Much maligned, giant clams are in fact real 'pearls'

The giant clam (*Tridacna gigas*) of the coral reefs of the Indian and Pacific oceans hold the world record for the largest mollusc with a live shell. A specimen measuring 110 centimetres across and weighing 233 kilograms was found off the Japanese island of Ishigaki. Another giant clam (230 kilograms and 132 centimetres across) can be seen in the American Museum of Natural History in New York.

THE WORLD'S LARGEST PEARL

The giant clam, one metre across and weighing 250 kilograms, is the world's largest bivalve. Its heavily ridged shell was once used for bowls and fonts. Perhaps the most famous of these is the huge font in the Church of Saint-Sulpice in Paris, France, presented to François I, king of France (1515–47), by the Doge of Venice. Its valves measure 91 centimetres and weigh 260 kilograms. The largest pearl on record was found in a giant clam in the early 1930s near the Philippines. It weighs almost 7 kilograms.

The shell of the giant clam is often decorated with a variety of different coloured organisms. The tiny unicellular seaweed (*Zooxanthellae*) that grows along the edges of the shell could almost be said to be cultivated by the clam. This association is mutually beneficial since, in return for food from the clam, the seaweed provides it with an additional supply of oxygen.

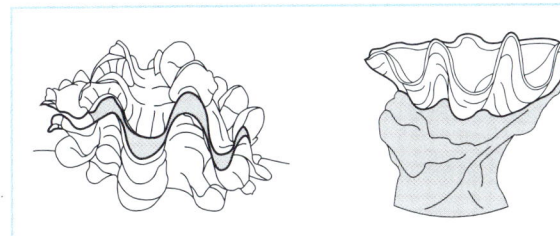

For several hundred years, the valves of giant clams have been imported into Europe to be used as fonts in churches.

Jaws or giant clamp?

The fact that a giant clam can trap a human being in its valves has earned it a reputation as a killer. In fact, it is by nature a harmless filter that feeds off marine micro-organisms. The only threat is posed by its defense mechanism – a single but powerful muscle that closes the shell – and the fact that it is well camouflaged by the surrounding coral.

If disturbed, the clam can be dangerous since it reacts by closing its shell and trapping the intruder. So be warned – don't put your finger or hand inside a giant clam. If you do get trapped, it's no use reacting like a scalded cat. The only way to escape from these impressive jaws is to cut through the adductor muscle or break the shell. However, since the clam closes fairly slowly, intruders can usually escape provided they keep their cool.

Found exclusively on the coral reefs of the Indian and Pacific oceans, the giant clam is much sought after for its flesh and its shell, which is made into church fonts, garden ornaments, souvenirs and even tools. Although the trade in these huge molluscs is now illegal, their survival hangs in the balance.

Hunted for their highly prized horns, rhinoceroses are the last survivors of a prehistoric age

Rhinoceroses – from Greek rhino (nose) and keras (horn) – use their horns to test the strength and reflexes of their adversaries.

A PREHISTORIC SWORDSMAN

The white rhinoceros (*Ceralotherium simum*) is the world's second largest mammal after the elephant. It measures between 1.5 and 1.85 metres at the shoulder and weighs between 2.3 and 3.6 tonnes. Although the black rhinoceros (*Diceros bicornis*) is about the same height (1.5 metres), it only weighs 1.8 tonnes. Another difference between these two rhinoceroses – rather than their colour which is in fact the same – is the shape of their mouth. The white rhino has a broad, straight mouth ideally adapted for grazing ('white' is a distortion of the Afrikaans word meaning 'wide'). Confrontations between these giants follow a predetermined pattern as, with much snorting and spraying of urine, they cross horns in an attempt to intimidate their rival.

Rhinoceroses are born without horns, which only grow when the calf is two or three years old. During this period, they cannot defend themselves against predators and therefore stay close to their mother for the first few years of their life. Her impressive bulk and formidable horns offer protection until the calf's own horns have developed.

A rhino's feet have to be able to support its great weight. The rhinoceros is a member of the order of Perissodactyla, odd-toed ungulates in which the main weight-bearing axis of the foot passes through a single toe. In the case of the rhinoceros (which has three toes), it is the central toe that bears the weight.

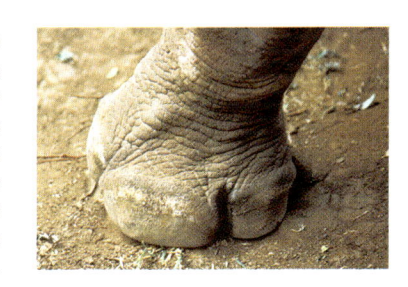

The territory of the white rhinoceros is much less extensive than that of the black rhino. It is a less solitary and more territorial creature. The males, sometimes as many as five per square kilometre, mark their territory with droppings and urine. Confrontations always follow the same pattern, with the males crossing horns like swordsmen testing each other's strength and reflexes.

Dangerous horn, endangered species

The white rhinoceros has two horns which, like our own nails and hair, are composed of keratin. They have no bony core and are not attached to the skull. If they break off, they grow back in two to three years. The phallic shape of their horns and their great sexual energy (rhinoceroses mate for an hour at a time and several times a day) have led to rhino horns being invested with aphrodisiac properties. Although analyses have not revealed anything other than keratin, recent research has shown that the absorption of rhinoceros horn by the human body can result in lesions characteristic of the highly infectious disease, anthrax. In spite of this, the great demand for rhinoceros horn led to the mass slaughter of these animals. Today, the few remaining survivors live in game reserves.

Profile

White rhinoceros
Ceraltherium simum
Family: Rhinocerotidae
Size: 1.5 m to 1.85 m at the shoulder
Weight: 2.3 tonnes to 3.6 tonnes Distinguishing features: two horns; front horn (longer than the back) 65 cm (55 cm for the black rhino)
Distribution: Africa, from Lake Chad to the White Nile – 800 individuals in Chad, Democratic Republic of Congo (formerly Zaire), Uganda, Sudan, Central African Republic in 1980 – and especially South Africa and Zimbabwe
Diet: herbivorous
Gestation period: approximately 460 days
Life expectancy: 40 to 50 years

Although smaller than the white rhinoceros and only moderately aggressive towards other rhinos, the black rhinoceros (*Diceros bicornis*) is much more likely to attack other animals and humans. It will charge at full tilt, without warning and apparently without provocation, and even attacks peaceable – and much larger – elephants.

The rhino's impressive and distinctive outline appears in many prehistoric cave drawings. However, it is an outline that is in danger of disappearing from the grasslands of tropical Africa. Rhinoceroses became the victims of the aphrodisiac properties attributed to their horns by Eastern and Western societies and were slaughtered throughout Africa and Asia. Today the few survivors live in game reserves.

Despite being the largest members of the shark family
whale sharks
are non-aggressive plankton-eaters

These impressive sharks tend to be seen in the open sea, where they usually swim near the surface.

PLANKTON-EATERS RATHER THAN MAN-EATERS

Not all the 350 recorded species of shark live up to their fearful reputation. The great white shark (*Carcharodon carcharias*), under 8 metres long and weighing around 3 tonnes, heads the list of dangerous sharks. By contrast, the much larger whale shark (*Rhiniodon typus*) – 12 metres long and weighing 10 tonnes – eats nothing but plankton. Although this marine mastodon is the largest known shark and – except for some whales – the world's largest animal, it is completely harmless. It huge mouth is only used to strain plankton and krill (its staple diet) from the water.

Whale sharks are non-aggressive and completely harmless. They are also very trusting and quite happy in the presence of divers. The only risk run by divers is being caught a glancing blow by the huge tail. They would also be well advised to avoid contact with the shark's extremely rough skin, as the sharp surface will cut a person's skin if it is not protected by gloves or a wet suit.

TOOTH-LIKE SCALES

The peaceable whale shark is much more widely found than the smaller but terrifying white shark with its deadly jaws. Whale sharks generally live near the surface in warm tropical waters and are undisturbed by the approach of boats or divers. Divers have nothing to fear from these non-aggressive creatures, provided they do not inadvertently collide with their massive bulk or 'rub them up the wrong way'. The shark's skin is encrusted with millions of tiny tooth-like scales which are extremely abrasive.

Profile

Whale shark
Rhiniodon typus
Size: 12 m (record 18.6 m)
Weight: up to 13 tonnes
Habitat: usually near the surface in the middle of the great ocean basins or near the coasts of temperate or tropical seas
Diet: organisms filtered out of the water
Reproduction: Oviparous (eggs hatched outside the body) and ovoviviparous (eggs hatched inside the body)
Distinguishing features: broad, flat head; truncated snout; large gill openings; dark back with white spots and vertical white lines

About 3 tonnes of water an hour pass through this mouth with its 3000 tiny teeth. The whale shark swims with its mouth wide open, swallowing vast quantities of water from which it strains plankton and other tiny organisms. It also devours the small crustaceans, mackerel and young tuna caught up in the eddies created by its huge mouth.

One hump or two, **camels** are faithful companions in the desert

At birth, baby camels weigh between 25 and 50 kilograms and measure 1.2 metres at their hump. The day after they are born, they are able to follow their mother as she grazes or join the herd, resting and feeding when the herd stops. They are often weaned by the herdsmen who also need the camel's milk. Males are mature at the age of four or five, and females at three or four.

DROMEDARY OR CAMEL?

The term camel is applied to the 17 million animals of the genus Camelus found throughout the world. However, 90 percent of these are in fact dromedaries found mainly in North Africa. The dromedary (or Arabian camel) is easily recognised by its single hump, long curved neck and long legs. The Bactrian camel – found in central Asia, from Turkey to Mongolia – is heavier and smaller. It stands up to 1.8 metres at the shoulder and weighs between 500 and 700 kilograms. The dromedary is ten times more resistant than humans and four times more resistant than the donkey to the heat of the desert, while its Asian counterpart easily survives winter temperatures as low as –25°C.

The two-humped Bactrian camel of Asia and the single-humped dromedary of North Africa have been domesticated for centuries. In central Asia, camels cross snowy mountain passes carrying loads of almost 300 kilograms. In the deserts of Africa and the Near East, dromedaries carry loads of around 100 kilograms and can go up to a month without water.

The slightly pendulous lower lip and characteristic head carriage, with its nostrils above its eyes, give the camel a haughty expression.

Profile

Dromedary
Camelus dromedarius
Family: Camelidae
Size: 1.7 m to 2.1 m at the shoulder (up to 2.3 m at the hump)
Length: approximately 3 m (head and body)
Weight: 400 kg to 700 kg (females weigh less than males)
Habitat: deserts and semi-deserts, from the Sahara to India
Diet: herbivore
Gestation period: 13 months
Life expectancy: 30 to 40 years
Predators: mainly lions

TOLERANCE AND ADAPTABILITY

Camels are remarkably adaptable. Their coat insulates them against winter cold and summer heat, they can close their nostrils to prevent water evaporation, they carry energy reserves in their hump, and their split upper lip enables them to eat even the spikiest twigs. They are the only animals to tolerate with equanimity an internal body temperature that varies between 34°C at night and 41°C in the day. Extremely resistant to dehydration, they can go for a number of days without drinking and lose up to 20 percent of their body water without suffering harmful physical effects (humans die if they lose 12 percent).

'Ships of the desert'

Camels are found from the western Sahara to India, as well as in Australia where a camel population introduced in the 19th century is today living in the wild. Bactrian camels are found in Afghanistan, Iran and China, and several hundred wild camels still live in the Gobi Desert.
In Asia, a camel is said to be worth 8 yaks, 9 horses or 45 sheep. In the desert, camels are the mainstay of nomadic life, enabling herdsmen to move on in search of grazing for their sheep and goats. They carry equipment and belongings, provide food in the form of milk and meat, and their hair and hide are used for a variety of purposes. At walking pace, they can cover 40 kilometres a day at an average speed of 3.5 kilometres an hour. Although they can travel at up to 25 kilometres per hour, they cannot maintain this speed for long.

The dromedary's single hump is always vertical, but varies in height depending on the amount of food available.

From tiny hatchlings to marine giants, **leatherback turtles** fight a constant battle for survival

THE LARGEST AND MOST MYSTERIOUS OF TURTLES

The leatherback turtle is the largest tortoise in the world, far bigger even than the giant Galápagos tortoise, one of the largest terrestrial tortoises. Their shell can be as much as 1.92 metres long and they weigh an average of 400 kilograms, with some old individuals weighing around a tonne. These descendants of primitive reptiles have gradually developed the characteristics needed to survive in a marine environment: enlarged forelimbs that have evolved into long 'oars', highly developed pectoral muscles and short paddle-like hind legs that act as rudders. Unlike other marine tortoises, leatherback turtles live in the open sea. Their speed and stamina enable them to cover thousands of kilometres in only a few weeks, swimming alternately underwater and on the surface (they come up for air every four minutes or so). It is extremely difficult to observe these excellent swimmers as they only come near the shore to hunt and nest. It is often still dark when the females return to the sea after laying their eggs.

Profile

Leathery turtle
Dermochelys coriacea
Family: Dermochelidae
Size: 1.1 m to 1.92 m
Weight: 400 kg (average); 27 g to 55 g at birth
Habitat: the open sea in all warm oceans, from the surface to a depth of 1200m
Diet: fish, molluscs, crustaceans, seaweed and especially jellyfish
Life expectancy: not known
Number: approx. 120,000 adult females
Life expectancy: up to 40 years

The leatherback (or leathery) turtle is immediately recognizable by its huge size and total absence of scales and claws. Its name derives from its pseudo-shell which looks like shiny blue-black leather. This leathery carapace (about 4 centimetres thick) consists of thousands of tiny articulated nodules covered with a fine, shiny skin.

Eggs are laid in the bare sand along the centre of the beach. This ideal location is exposed to the sun, far enough from the sea to prevent the nest being flooded and far enough from vegetation on the beach's upper edge to prevent eggs being destroyed by roots.

As she lay her eggs, the female turtle sheds 'false tears'. These are in fact a slimy liquid that lubricates her eyes and protects them from the grains of sand.

Born in the sand

Although they spend most of their life swimming in the open sea, leatherback turtles lay their eggs on land. The female usually comes ashore at night, using the same beach each time she lays her eggs. Having first 'swept' the sand, she spends almost half an hour digging a hole (about 80 centimetres deep) and the next ten minutes laying a pile of about a hundred eggs, each 5 centimetres in diameter. After filling in the hole, she 'sweeps' the nest area once more and returns to the sea. Between two and three months later, the baby turtles break through the membranous 'shell' of the egg with the little hooked 'beak' of their snout. It takes the newly hatched turtles between three and four days to make their way through the sand – without air or water – from the nest to the surface. They usually emerge into the world for the first time in the late afternoon, when the heat of the sun is less dangerous. They reach the sea by following the natural slope of the beach, attracted by the shining surface of the water.

The female turtle arrives on the beach at night and 'chooses' her nest site. She uses her hind legs to dig her nest in which she then lays her eggs two or three at a time.

The eggs usually hatch after two to three months. It takes the baby turtles, each weighing between 27 and 55 grams at birth, three to four days to dig their way out of the nest. They then make their way to the sea, but few actually reach their destination as many predators are partial to these tiny hatchlings with their tender 'shells' which are in fact a leathery carapace rather than a hard, bony shell.

With their bald heads and long dark wings
marabou storks
look like mournful undertakers

An unprepossessing appearance

These tall birds often have a wingspan of almost 3 metres, with a record (a marabou shot in central Africa, in 1934) of 4 metres. Their huge, powerful beaks are used to tear open the stomach wall of the carcasses on which they feed. A bald head and large, drooping pouch beneath the throat complete the rather unprepossessing appearance of this 'vulture stork' that shares its macabre fare with hyenas and other vultures.

Tail feathers were its downfall

The soft, downy feathers from beneath the tail of this large wading bird were once much sought after for trimming ladies' garments. This contributed to the decrease in the marabou population.

The long-sighted marabou stork can 'spot a carcass a mile off', while its sharp beak enables it to spear fish, rats and even flamingoes.

Marabous are members of the large stork family (Ciconiidae). They live in colonies in the sub-Saharan regions and also gravitate around towns and villages where they are attracted by household waste. Although protected by international law, they are becoming increasingly rare in South Africa due to the destruction of their habitat.

Profile

Marabou stork
Leptoptilos crumeniferus
Family: Ciconiidae

Size: 1.4 m
Wingspan: approx. 3 m (record 4.06 m)
Weight: around 5 kg
Habitat: nests in colonies on trees and rocks in semi-arid zones. It often takes advantage of human activity and gravitates around towns, fishing villages, cattle farms and rubbish tips
Diet: mainly carrion
Incubation period: around 30 days
Number of eggs per brood: 2 or 3

A 'cleaner' with a healthy appetite

Just as the Andean condor (*Vultur gryphus*) is known as the 'cleaner' of the Andes mountains of South America, so the marabou stork is the 'cleaner' of the African savanna, as well as its towns and villages. This carrion-eating bird needs to eat 720 grams of food every day and it majestic flight enables it to spot the carcasses on which it feeds. In fact the marabou is omnivorous and will eat absolutely anything, from all kinds of carcasses, fish and young crocodiles to termites and even household rubbish.

The marabou's long pointed beak and long legs give it a strange gait which emphasizes its rather disturbing appearance as it strides across the savanna.

In flight, these huge birds — with their large black wings, short tail and their neck pulled in — look like the vultures with which they share their meals. Like vultures, marabou storks are almost bald, which is an advantage when sticking their heads inside large carcasses.

Primeval in appearance, giant lizards look disturbingly like dragons

THE KOMODO DRAGON, A PREHISTORIC MONSTER

The Komodo dragon or monitor, found only on the Indonesian island of Komodo, is an extremely impressive and imposing creature. In 1912, the director of the Buitenzorg botanical gardens (Java) was informed of the existence of giant 'land crocodiles' and managed to capture four Komodo dragons and bring them back alive. These strange creatures caused such a sensation that reports of specimens of up to 7 metres were widely believed, until it was realised that this was a slight exaggeration! However, these lizards can grow to a length of 3 metres and can weigh as much as 135 kilograms.

Monitor lizards can swallow large prey by opening their jaws very wide.

The grey-black scales and forked tongue of the huge Komodo monitor give it a sinister appearance. These monsters have always inspired fear and may well have served as the model for the dragons of legend and mythology.

The monitor's powerful legs enable it to move extremely rapidly, while its razor-sharp teeth and sharp claws can inflict grave wounds. Once it spots its prey, the monitor pursues it, seizes it in its jaws and kills it by shaking it and striking it against the ground or any other hard object.

A life of leisure

The common iguana (*Iguana iguana*) is a rather lazy creature. It spends 96 percent of its time resting, 3 percent breeding and 1 percent feeding. It should be said that to feed, this idle monster – which loves to bask in the sun when it is not resting in the trees – hardly needs to move. Adults are entirely herbivorous (the young sometimes eat insects) and its meals consist of a mouthful of vegetation. Its pointed, close-set teeth are only used to cut and tear the leaves and fruit that constitute its daily fare.

The iguana loves to bask in the sun. It does this on the ground, in thickets or the branches of mimosas.

THE COMMON IGUANA, A HARMLESS 'MONSTER'

This exclusively American lizard, which seems to have emerged from the depths of time, is the largest member of the iguana family. It can grow to 2 metres in length and weigh up to 5 kilograms. With its hooked claws, long tail (used in self defence and for swimming), spiny dorsal crest, pendulous cheeks and the flaccid, inflatable pocket of skin beneath its throat (the gular pouch), this tree-dwelling dragon looks diabolical. However, it is completely harmless.

This large, peaceable lizard with its spiny scales and long hooked claws, spends most of its time lying in trees, its bronze eyes ever watchful. It seems to 'thumb its nose' at the hustle and bustle of the modern world from the depths of time. Although its fantastical appearance is somewhat alarming, its herbivorous diet consists solely of leaves, fruit and – most importantly – sun.

With their slender bodies and beautiful mottled coats, giraffes are the supermodels of the savanna

An elegant heavyweight

Once, vast herds of giraffe populated Africa, from the shores of the Mediterranean in the north to the tip of South Africa. In the 19th century, they were decimated by hunters and today live in small, protected communities on the grassy and wooded plains south of the Sahara: Senegal, Mauritania, the regions bordering the River Niger and Cameroon.
In spite of their slender proportions, giraffes – with a body weight of between 800 and 1000 kilograms – are among the world's heaviest land mammals. They are also the world's tallest animals and can measure over 6 metres from the ground to the tip of their horns, with their head and neck accounting for almost half their total height. They never exceed 3.3 metres at the shoulder.

The giraffe's neck consists of seven enlarged cervical vertebrae, each measuring almost 40 centimetres.

> ### High-level dining
> The evergreen foliage of the acacia (*Acacia xanthophloea*), rich in proteins and sugars, grows at a height of between 2 and 6 metres from the ground. It provides a rich source of aerial grazing which, without the giraffe, would go to waste. Because they graze superficially on a limited number of leaves, giraffes do not damage the vegetation but actually promote growth.

Fights between males occur throughout the year, regardless of whether or not there are females present. The process is known as 'necking' since they mainly use their necks. The victor establishes his supremacy by mounting his rival in a simulated act of copulation. 'Necking' is therefore an integral part of the giraffe's sexual and social life.

The structure of a group of giraffes varies from day to day. They appear to consist of an association of individuals formed to provide protection against predators.

Zebras and giraffes can happily share the same biotope (a small area that supports a particular community) as they have different food requirements. Zebras also feel more secure in the presence of giraffes, since each member of a group of giraffes surveys a particular point on the horizon and gives the alert if they see a predator.

Although all giraffes have horns, some males develop another pair of bony projections behind their horns and a single projection on their nose.

At a leisurely pace a giraffe moves at about 7 kilometres an hour over flat, open areas. The front and hind leg on the same side of the body move together or, to be more precise, the front leg leaves the ground immediately after the hind leg. This distinctive gait enables big strides to be taken and prevents the long legs from becoming entangled. A galloping giraffe can reach speeds of up to 56 kilometres an hour.

Drinking is something of a gymnastic feat for a giraffe.

Profile

Giraffe
Giraffa camelopardalis
Family: Giraffidae
Size: 5.3 m (average male); 3.3 m at the shoulder
Weight: 800 kg to 1300 kg
Habitat: African savanna, wooded grassland
Diet: herbivore
Gestation period: 15 months
Number of young: usually 1
Life expectancy: 26 years
Predators: lions and humans
Distinguishing features: mottled coat (reddish-brown markings on beige ground); very long neck; world's tallest land mammal

A LARGE BABY

Birth can be traumatic for a baby giraffe. Because the female stands to 'drop' her young, the baby's first encounter with the ground is from a height of almost 2 metres. In spite of this rather sudden aerial birth, the baby stands on its very shaky legs barely half an hour later. After an hour, it follows its mother and, after about ten hours, it runs about. As giraffes usually give birth at dawn, the baby is fairly mobile by nightfall with its attendant predators. At three days old, the baby is strong enough to jump.

At birth, giraffes stand about 2 metres high and weigh between 50 and 70 kilograms. During the first month of their life, young giraffes grow at a rate of 23 centimetres a week. If they survive until their first birthday (the mortality rate among giraffes during the first year often exceeds 50 percent), they will leave their mother when they are 16 months old. Female giraffes 'drop' their first baby at the age of five, after 15 months' gestation. Under the right conditions, they produce a baby every 18 months until the age of 20.

A rush of blood to the head

When a giraffe drinks, it spreads its front legs, bends its knees and moves its head backwards and forwards at an increasingly rapid rate and in a wider and wider arc until it comes into contact with the water. It drinks between 10 and 15 litres of water at one go. When the giraffe lowers its head, its brain is suddenly 2 metres below its heart. To prevent the brain being flooded by the sudden rush of blood, blood vessels channel some of it away and special valves in the wall of the jugular vein stop it flowing back into the brain.

Each baby giraffe has a different pattern of markings on the left side of its neck. Although they may darken, its markings will remain the same as it grows to adulthood.

Reputedly bad tempered, in reality
water buffaloes
are extremely gentle giants

The Indian (or Asian) buffalo has a greater need for water than its African cousin. It lives in the marshes and among the tall grasses near ricefields, feeding on aquatic plants and grasses. In the Kaziranga nature reserve, it lives peacefully alongside the single-horned Indian rhinoceros (*Rhinoceros unicornis*).

SPECIAL HORNS

The water buffalo or Indian buffalo can grow to a height of 1.8 metres at the shoulder and weigh almost a tonne. Males have long, semicircular horns that are backward curving and flattened at the front. Having been extensively hunted, especially by poachers for its meat and horns, this powerful member of the cattle family learnt to defend itself – thus a non-aggressive herbivore became renowned for its ferocity. It has been crossed with domestic buffalo to produce a smaller but more docile and resilient animal. This cross – used for riding and as a draught and pack animal – is well suited to work on the flood plains and in the ricefields.

Past experience and potential danger has made buffaloes extremely nervous when they are near water. They can consume their daily requirement of 30 litres of water in one go, in only six minutes! When they can drink at their leisure, they drink for one or two minutes at a time.

Profile

Indian (or water) buffalo
Bubalus arnee
Family: Bovidae

Size: 1 m to 1.8 m at the shoulder
Habitat: marshes and tall grasses near rivers; in central India, they live in drier, forest areas interspersed with clearings, rivers and pools
Diet: varied herbivorous diet, mainly grazing (grass, leaves, buds)
Gestation period: 330 days
Number of young: 1
Weight at birth: 26 kg to 50 kg
Life expectancy: 20 years (maximum) in the wild

In prehistoric times, the water buffalo or Indian buffalo was found from the Indian peninsula to Asia, as well as in North Africa. Today, it is endangered and – unlike its African cousins the Cape buffalo (*Synercus caffer*) and pygmy buffalo – is a protected species. Few Indian buffalo live entirely in the wild, at most 1000 in the whole of India and Nepal, and about 40 in Thailand, while Burma, Indochina, Malaysia, Sri Lanka and Borneo have only a few scattered pockets of wild buffalo.

The Indian buffalo is extremely courageous and is a dangerous prey for tigers. Before charging, it paws the ground, lowers its head and gives a powerful bellow. Tigers avoid adult buffaloes and tend to attack the young. In certain circumstances, wild buffalo may even attack domestic elephants ridden by their mahout (elephant driver).

Fascinating and elusive, giant squid have the largest eyes in the animal kingdom

Octopus or squid? A legendary monster

Although octopuses are often imaginatively described as huge, terrifying sea monsters, the largest known species (*Octopodus dofleini*), which inhabits the shores of the North Pacific, is no more than 3 metres in length and weighs around 50 kilograms. The 'monsters' described could in fact be giant squid, legendary creatures once known as octopuses, that live deep in the ocean at between 300 and 1000 metres below the surface. Even if the terrifying tales about them are somewhat exaggerated, they do contain a grain of truth since giant squid have been known to attack boats, probably mistaking them for sperm whales, their sworn enemies.

10-metre tentacles

Generally speaking, squid are extremely resilient swimmers. Their torpedo-shaped body, with its large fins and ten sucker-bearing tentacles, enables them to swim at great speed. The combined length of their body and tentacles, produce some impressive dimensions. Some species, *Architeuthis princeps*, for instance, has an incredibly long body – almost 6.5 metres with tentacles measuring 10 metres – and weighs up to 3 tonnes. The largest squid on record was captured in 1993 off the coast of New Zealand. Its body measured 8 metres and its tentacles 14 metres – an overall length of 22 metres! The most commonly found species in the North Atlantic, *Architeuthis dux*, usually only measures between 1 and 2 metres, although a closely related species (*Architeuthis clarkei*), washed up on the east coast of England, had an overall length of 6 metres.

The great unkown

The giant squid has never been observed in its natural environment. The only known specimens are those washed ashore or caught up in fishing nets. Storms and deadly combats between squid and sperm whales mean that the squid's soft body is severely damaged before it reaches the surface or shore, and they can only be identified by the shape of their jaw. An examination of the stomach contents of sperm whales has also provided more information on these creatures. The discovery of suckers with a diameter of 25 centimetres confirmed the existence of a squid with a body

Eyes the size of basket balls

The giant squid's only predator is the sperm whale which is particularly fond of its soft flesh. Although these whales feed almost entirely on the smaller cephalopods (between 1 and 2 metres), they can also deal with much bigger prey. An entire squid, weighing 200 kilograms and with tentacles over 10 metres long, was found in the stomach of a sperm whale caught off the Azores. The whale that swallowed this giant mollusc was itself only 14.5 metres long. The eyes of a giant squid found in the stomach of another sperm whale proved to be the largest eyes in the animal kingdom. With a diameter of 40 centimetres, they were the size of basket balls

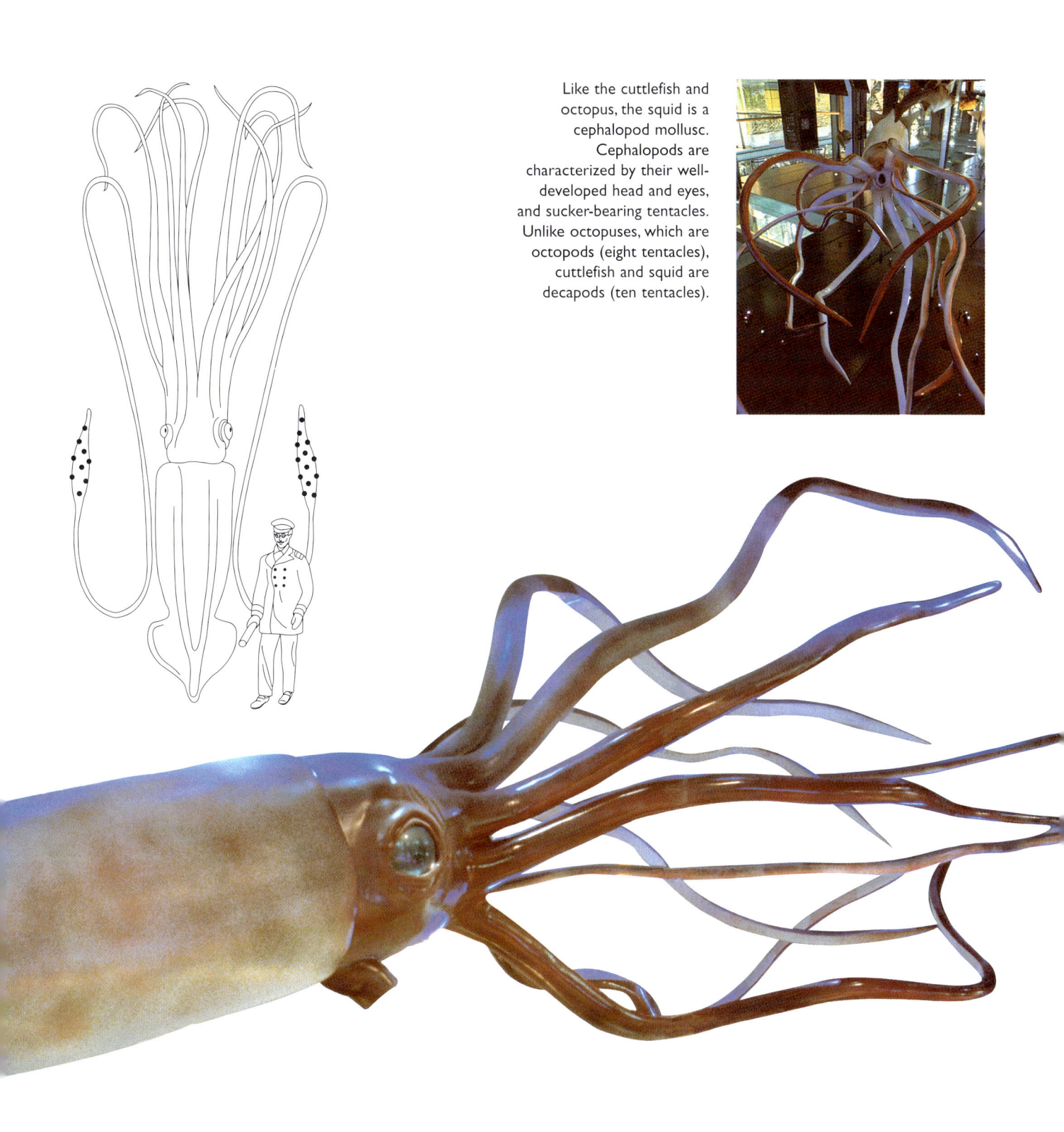

Like the cuttlefish and octopus, the squid is a cephalopod mollusc. Cephalopods are characterized by their well-developed head and eyes, and sucker-bearing tentacles. Unlike octopuses, which are octopods (eight tentacles), cuttlefish and squid are decapods (ten tentacles).

length of over 10 metres and an overall length (including tentacles) of 25 metres. This would suggest a body weight of several tonnes!

SEA MONSTERS VERSUS SPERM WHALES

These tentacled monsters with their all-too-easily imaginable deadly embrace are nevertheless the prey of a species much bigger and stronger than themselves: sperm whales (*Physeter catodon*). When a sperm whale encounters a giant squid it leaps from the water, twisting and turning and striking the surface of the water to rid itself of this 'clinging' mollusc whose hooked suckers inflict terrible wounds. However, recent research has shown that squid suffocate in temperatures above 6°C. Therefore, when the sperm whale rises to the surface, it is effectively suffocating the squid.

With their power, strength and aerobatic skills, bald eagles are real high fliers

An impressive wingspan

The bald (or American) eagle (*Haliaeetus leucocephalus*) grows to between 71 and 96 centimetres in length and has a truly impressive wingspan of up to 2.4 metres! With an average weight of 5.3 kilograms, the females tend to be larger than the males, which do not exceed 4 kilograms. Young eagles in fact have a greater wingspan than their older counterparts, an unusual characteristic that is probably explained by the difference in behaviour and lifestyle. Bald eagles are more erratic and migratory when young and therefore have greater need of this large wingspan in the early years of their life.

A two-tonne nest!

After dazzling mating displays involving some remarkable aerobatics and vocal exercises, the eagles pair off and go about building their nests. These have to be situated near an abundant supply of food and strategically located vantage points. Because bald eagles often repair and strengthen the previous year's nest by adding a layer of branches, their nests can become quite large. A nest destroyed during a storm after 36 years' use was found to be 3 metres across, 6 metres thick and weigh almost 2 tonnes!

Bald eagles are extremely accomplished fishers. Having spotted their prey from a great distance, they swoop down and scoop it up from the surface of the water, barely getting their toes wet.

The bald eagle's impressive beak is only used for tearing up its prey. Its feet – with their short toes and long, hooked talons – are what rank it among the world's super-predators. Its talons slip easily through water and slice into the flesh of the fish that form the basis of its diet. The fleshy, non-slip pads beneath its toes enable it to catch even the slipperiest customers.

With its piercing yellow eyes and strong hooked beak, the head of the bald eagle reflects the characteristic determination of this magnificent bird of prey.

Although extremely territorial during the mating season, bald eagles become much more sociable in winter when they roost happily together in an attempt to combat wind and cold. They also form groups to hunt mammals and birds.

The bald eagle, which inhabits the coasts, lakes and rivers of North America, was so called by the early settlers because of the adult's characteristic white head. Although considered 'majestic and noble' by some and 'lazy and thieving' by others, it is nevertheless an impressive and powerful bird of prey. Today, it is the emblem of the United States.

In spite of their corpulent bodies, crocodiles are not big eaters

Living on an empty stomach

Along with the reticulate python and the anaconda, the African crocodile is one of the world's largest reptiles. It also shares the distinction of being one of the heaviest with the leathery turtle. However, in spite of growing to almost 8 metres in length, crocodiles are not big eaters and only feed about 50 times a year. They store the energy provided by their food in a much more efficient way than other animals: about 60 percent of the food absorbed is stored in the fleshy part of their tail, their abdomen and along their back. Old crocodiles can live for up to two years without feeding!

The larger crocodiles tend to eat during the hot summer months, feeding on birds, fish, mammals (buffalo, zebra, antelope) and carcasses which they locate by the smell. During the colder months, their digestive process slows down and only the smaller crocodiles feed, mainly on insects.

Profile

African crocodile
Crocodylus niloticus
Family: Crocodylidae
Size: 4.5 m (record: 7.9 m)
Weight: up to 1 tonne
Distribution: southern Sahara to Lesotho, Madagascar and the Comoro Islands
Habitat: fresh water, rivers, lakes, swamps, occasionally river estuaries and coastal mangrove swamps
Diet: a widely varied carnivorous diet (mammals, reptiles, amphibians, fish, birds, insects, spiders)
Life expectancy: up to 100 years

In spite of their great size, crocodiles can move rapidly and easily on land, especially when they abandon their characteristic crawling gait and raise themselves up on all fours. They can move at a sort of gallop, maintaining a speed of 17 kilometres an hour over a distance of several kilometres.

The prehistoric-looking crocodile, with its impressive armour plating, is a distant relative of the dinosaur. Its only enemies are human beings and other crocodiles. Crocodiles live in communities dominated by the largest and most aggressive males. There is a strict hierarchy and conflicts are few and far between.

AN ADVOCATE OF 'LEAST EFFORT'

Generally speaking, crocodiles avoid making any form of unnecessary effort. They prefer to hunt on the edge of a river or lake where their potential prey often slips on the steep bank or in the mud as it drinks at the water's edge. The crocodile lies in wait, often for days at a time, its long body submerged and motionless. It is skilled in the art of camouflage and only its eyes and nostrils are visible. When an antelope or buffalo ventures on to the muddy bank to drink, the crocodile slips silently forward and seizes the leg or muzzle of its prey in its powerful jaws, pulling it off balance, or dazes it with a blow from its heavy head. It then drags the animal into the water to drown it before tearing it apart and swallowing the pieces, even the bones, without chewing them. If the animal is too heavy for one crocodile to move, it calls upon other members of the group to help.

When a crocodile goes fishing on its own, it swims slowly, curving its tail so that its body forms an arc. Then, with a quick sideways movement of its flat snout, it catches and swallows small fish whole. It swallows larger fish by lifting its head vertically.

Large eggs ...small crocodiles

Before laying eggs, a female crocodile digs a series of holes on dry land. They will contain 30 to 50 eggs, each weighing 40 to 60 grams. Three months later, the eggs hatch and baby crocodiles emerge. These tiny creatures are about 28 centimetres long and weigh 500 grams. The female does not help them break their shell, but she does protect them after hatching as they risk being eaten by larger predators.

They grow at a rate of 30 centimetres a year until they are sexually mature at the age of 12 to 15.

THE GAVIAL:
A SLENDER SNOUT ON WEAK LEGS

The 22 species of crocodilians that exist in the world today are divided into three main families: crocodiles (14 species found in America, Africa and Asia), alligators (Mississippi, China) and caiman (Central and South America), while the gavial forms a separate family (Gavialidae).

The gavial can grow up to 7 metres in length. It has a very distinctive fine, cylindrical snout, a feature shared with the false gavial (*Tomistoma schlegeli*) from south-east Asia. Its leg muscles are so weak that it cannot raise its body off the ground or move on land. However, the gavial is extremely agile in water.

Saving their skin

For a long time, the gavial had nothing to fear from humans since it was dedicated to the Hindu god Vishnu (the Preserver or Sustainer) and therefore considered sacred. Today, it shares the fate of the African crocodile (once venerated by the Egyptians) and has become the victim of poachers who hunt it for its skin. The dramatic decrease in the numbers of some species of crocodile has led to the banning and/or control of their slaughter in the wild. However, in spite of the 100 or so crocodile farms and ranches worldwide that supply skins to the leather trade, the poaching still continues. The Zoological Society of New York estimates that the international leather trade is responsible for the death of some two million crocodiles, caiman and alligators each year…

Human beings are strong enough to wedge open a crocodile's jaws with their bare hands since its jaw muscles are not particularly well developed. This unwary antelope, on the other hand, was not quick enough to escape the trap. As well as being a 'super-predator', the crocodile is also a great 'cleaner' and plays a key role in maintaining the ecological balance.

Ivory tusks make **walruses** the 'elephants' of the Arctic

CLUMSY ON LAND, AGILE IN WATER

The walrus is certainly not as graceful as its cousin the sea lion! Its huge tailless body, weighing between 500 and 1300 kilograms, is covered with a thick layer of blubber and tough cinnamon-coloured skin. With its small head and enlarged upper canines, it looks rather like a deformed elephant. It forages in the mud and sediment on the seabed and, although extremely clumsy on land, it is perfectly adapted to life in the Arctic. It is remarkably agile in the water, reaching speeds of 35 kilometres an hour when pursuing its prey. It can remain under water for up to 30 minutes and dive to depths of 150 metres. It has great stamina and can swim for 250 kilometres at a stretch.

Walruses are extremely gregarious creatures and seek close bodily contact, to the point of being

In fine weather, great herds of walruses bask in the sun along the Arctic shores. These huge heaps of basking bodies often cover vast areas.

Profile

Walrus
Odobenus rosmarus
Family: Odobenidae

Size: up to 3.2 m
Weight: up to 1.5 tonnes
Habitat: Arctic waters, ice packs and floes, rocky coasts of Greenland and eastern Canada, as far as northern Eurasia and western Alaska
Diet: shellfish, small fish, shrimps and crabs
Gestation period: 15 to 16 months
Number of young: one (65 kg; 1.2 m)
Life expectancy: up to 40 years

Walruses have beautiful ivory tusks, – in fact extensions of the upper canines – which are very useful for cutting through ice and raking through mud foraging in the seabed, as well as being extremely dissuasive and effective weapons.

extremely promiscuous. As they lie one against – and often one on top of – the other, their thick skin acts as a protective shield that prevents them being injured by their neighbours' tusks.

ARMED TO THE TEETH

The walrus's tusks are common to both sexes. They are usually about 60 centimetres long – although they can be as much as a metre long in old males – and weigh between 3 and 6 kilograms. They are a useful indicator of the animal's age and sex: the tusks of the female are shorter, more slender and circular in cross section, while those of the male are heavier, straighter and longer, and elliptical in cross section. They pierce the gums when the young walrus is about six months old. By the time it is a year old, its 'tusks' measure about 2.5 centimetres but remain hidden by the fold of the lip until the age of two.

All for one and one for all

If a walrus is attacked by a polar bear, for example, the rest of the herd comes to its rescue with amazing alacrity, using their tusks like ice picks to drag their great weight towards the attacker. Would-be antagonists avoid getting too close to the great walrus herds and only attack isolated individuals. This mutual support system illustrates the great sense of group awareness among walruses. Bodily contact and communication by touch, scent and sound are extremely important to the species, in spite of the underlying aggression released by their sexual promiscuity and the power struggles between adult males.

Walruses use their great moustache, consisting of 450 whiskers, when searching the mud of the seabed for the clams and shellfish that form the basis of their diet. They are not averse to taking long breaks between dives and sometimes rest for as long as a week before returning to the water. Even so, they still manage to consume around 20 tonnes of shellfish a year!

Slow-moving and clumsy on land, hippopotamuses are extremely agile in water

UNGAINLY ON LAND

With their short, stumpy legs, disproportionately large head and hairless, barrel-shaped body, hippopotamuses have a very distinctive shape. They measure between 3 and 3.75 metres in length and 1.5 metres at the shoulder, and weigh between 1.4 and 2 tonnes, with a record male weighing in at 3.2 tonnes! They are naturally lazy and lead a tranquil life (30 to 40 years), their main exertion being to graze and yawn widely from time to time. On land, these slow-moving pachyderms seem disinclined to break any land speed records. However, they can – if the need arises and in spite of their great size – charge or flee at around 30 kilometres an hour.

...AT HOME IN THE WATER

Hippopotamuses spend their days – often motionless – in the water, and their nights on land. Although they move clumsily on land, they are extremely agile in water. They often move in a series of bursts of speed by propelling themselves along the river bed with their hind legs. They are also good swimmers. They do everything in the water, including sleeping and mating. When in the water, their high-placed nostrils enable them to breathe while remaining submerged.

Hippopotamuses love fresh (as opposed to salt) water, even when it is muddy or stagnant. They often stay submerged all day, protected from the sun. By remaining almost motionless, they conserve energy and maintain a constant body temperature.

Although their numbers are declining, hippopotamuses are found throughout Africa, from Sudan to South Africa and from the east to the west coast, wherever there are lakes and rivers. The region must be fairly wet, even during the dry season, to accommodate them all year round.

Hippos propel themselves in water using their hind legs, rather like frogs! When the water level is low, they look as if they are jumping along.

The hippo's nostrils, eyes and ears are positioned on top of its skull. As well as being able to breathe while remaining submerged, it can also smell, see and hear what is going on above the surface of the water.

The ancient Egyptians believed that hippopotamuses were the incarnation of the hippopotamus-goddess Taweret associated with women in childbirth. The young are always born in the wet season. They are lucky to survive their first year when infant mortality can be as high as 45 percent. But it is also a period of rapid growth, from 25 kilograms at birth to 250 kilograms at a year old!

In spite of their good-natured appearance, Kodiak bears are fierce animals who live by their strength

Kodiak bear cubs spend the first few months of their life in darkness. In spring, when they are about four months old, they emerge from the den where they were born. They stop suckling at about the same time and grow rapidly during the summer months. Their mother constantly calls her unruly and inquisitive youngsters to order and, if her warning growls are not enough to prevent them wandering off, she will give them a hefty cuff.

A GIANT OF A BEAR

Most brown bears stand about 1 metre high at the shoulder with a length of 2 metres. Their weight varies between 150 and 375 kilograms. Although the Russian bears of the Kamchatka Peninsula and the American grizzly are much bigger than this, the real giants live on the Alaskan islands, especially Kodiak Island to the south of Alaska. Kodiak bears stand up to 3.8 metres on their hind legs and weigh as much as 600 kilograms. When preparing for their winter fast, they eat up to 40 kilograms of food and put on almost 2.5 kilograms of fat a day. During the winter hibernation period, males lose almost 30 percent of their body weight and the females as much as 40 percent.

The female Kodiak shows her cubs – who often stay with her up to the age of 18 months – how to use their teeth and powerful claws to catch fish. The shoals of migrating fish provide a much richer source of protein and calories for brown bears than their usual diet which consists mainly of berries, tubers, roots and all kinds of fruit.

The cubs of this giant Alaskan bear are incredibly small and fragile. Although a female can give birth to as many as four cubs, there are usually two cubs in each litter. At birth, these 'cuddly' little bears weigh between 400 and 600 kilograms. It would take 500 cubs to equal the weight of their mother!

The Kodiak bear *(Ursus arctos middendorffi)* has a large, compact and powerfully built body. Although it often stands on its hind legs, it moves about on all fours. Its great size and weight prevent it indulging in major gymnastic feats, but it can climb, swim, jump and run and, if the need arises, it is capable of speeds of up to 50 kilometres an hour.

Creative workshop

*Having studied all of these creatures,
it's time to get creative.*

*All you need are a few odds and ends and a little ingenuity,
and you can incorporate some of the animals we've seen
into beautiful craft objects.*

*These simple projects will give you further insight into the
animal kingdom presented in the pages of this book.*

*An original and simple way to enjoy
the wonderful images of the animal kingdom.*

Polar bear cushion

Page 84

Giraffe picture

Page 86

Tiger tablecloth and napkins

Page 88

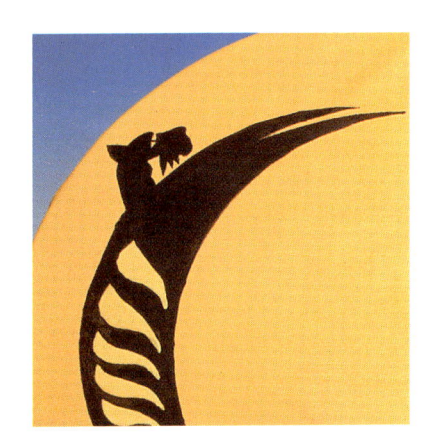

Snake velvet scarf

Page 90

Polar bear cushions

These tame polar bears will make a beautiful addition to your home.

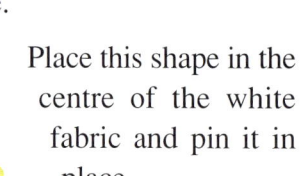

Preparing the pieces

Photocopy the designs of the polar bears, enlarging them to the required dimensions.

Reproduce these bears on tracing paper, outlining the back of the design with a soft black pencil.

Making the small cushion

Place the traced design on to the grey fabric, taping it down at all four corners. Trace the design on to the fabric.

Cut the fabric out around the outline.

Place this shape in the centre of the white fabric and pin it in place.

84

Sew around the edge of the design using close zigzag stitch.

Sew a hem on one long side of each of the two rectangles of white cotton fabric.

Assemble the three pieces of material, right sides together following the diagram and overlapping the two white pieces. Sew round all four sides of the square.

Turn the cover inside out and put the cushion into it.

Follow the same steps to make the large cushion.

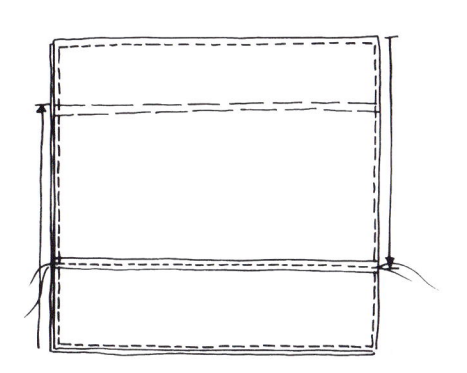

Materials

- three sheets of tracing paper • three cushion pads: two 65 centimetres square, one 40 centimetres square
- fabric for small cushion: a square of white cotton fabric and a square of grey cotton fabric, each 40 centimetres square, and two rectangular pieces of white cotton, 40 centimetres by 35 centimetres
- a sewing machine • pins
- a black pencil • a pair of scissors • adhesive tape

Giraffe picture

The acacia tree is the giraffe's favourite tree, which it grazes on 4 metres above the ground. This attractive picture is created using fabric offcuts and padded cardboard.

Preparing the backing

Photocopy the design, increasing it to fit the size of the padded cardboard. Place the photocopy on the cardboard, taping it in place at the four corners.

Draw the outline of the design with a sharp pencil to imprint it into the padded cardboard.

Using the Stanley knife, cut around the outline, about 3 to 5 millimetres deep.

Applying the fabric

Cut out the designs from the photocopy, to use as patterns.

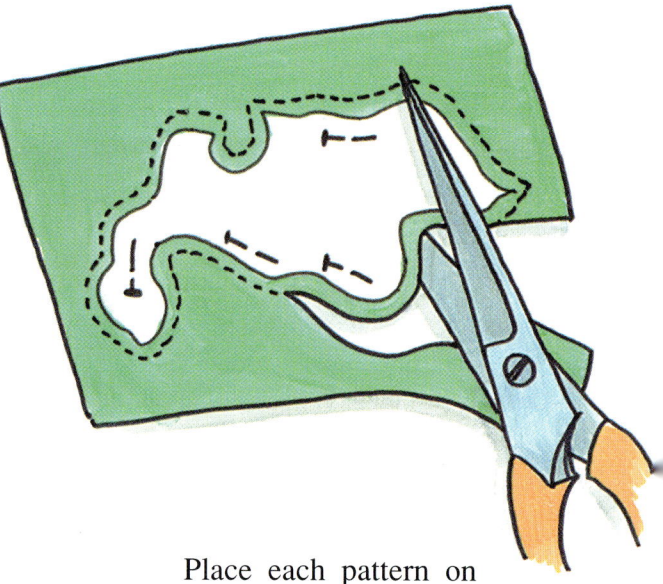

Place each pattern on to the material, wrong sides together, and cut round them, leaving 5 millimetres extra around the edges.

Position each piece of fabric on the picture. Using the metal nailfile, push the borders of the fabric into the incisions made with the Stanley knife.

You may need to practise this stage on an offcut of padded cardboard to perfect your technique.

To avoid wrinkles in the fabric, first push down one side of the fabric and then the other, to create tension.

Finishing

Draw on the giraffes' horns.

You can frame the picture in the same colour as one of the fabrics.

This technique can also be used for making other pictures.

Materials

- sheet of padded cardboard, 5 to 10 millimetres thick, white on both sides, of the size that you wish the picture to be • fabric scraps of various colours • a Stanley knife • a metal nailfile.

87

Tiger tablecloth and napkins

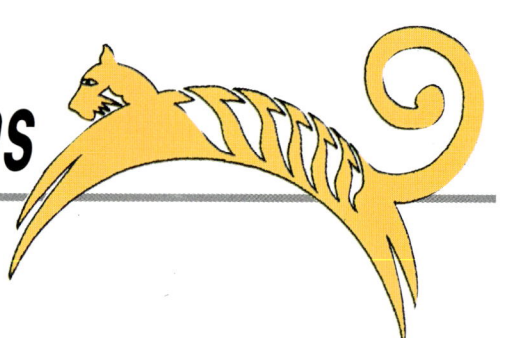

These stylized tigers will give life to a warm-coloured tablecloth.

Making the stencil

Photocopy the design of the tiger, increasing the size (42 centimetres for the cloth, 18 centimetres for the napkins).

Tape the stencil to the cardboard at the four corners. Cut out the shape of the tiger to make two stencils – one large and one small.

Stencilling the design

• **Tablecloth**

Take the fabric for the tablecloth, mark the centre and fold it into four. Place the stencil on the middle of the fabric so the design will form a circle around the centre of the tablecloth. Affix it at all four corners with adhesive tape.

For rectangular tablecloths: fold diagonally one way and then the other to find the centre. Place the stencil so the tiger is along the long side of the rectangle. The middle of the circle formed by the two tigers will be the centre of the cloth.

Using the stencil brush and undiluted paint, tap the paint on to the design. Do not let the paint seep behind the stencil.

Once the first tiger is complete, paint the second tiger on the other side of the tablecloth.

• **Napkins**

Stencil a small tiger in one corner of each napkin, with the tail of the design towards the centre, leaving 5 centimetres between the stencil and the edge of the fabric.

Fixing the colour

Iron the reverse side of the fabric to fix the fabric colour, following the manufacturer's instructions.

Finishing

Hem the tablecloth and napkins on four sides, using a fancy stitch for detail if you prefer.

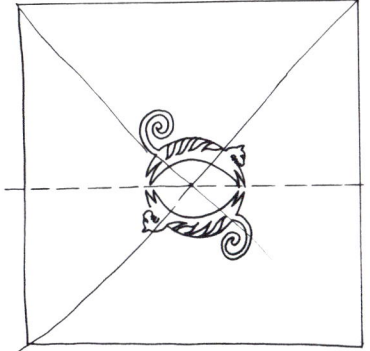

Materials

- a square of cotton fabric, 2 metres square (or a rectangle, depending on the shape of your table) and six squares of cotton fabric, 40 centimetres square • a sheet of cardboard, 56 centimetres by 65 centimetres, weight 250 grams • black fabric paint • adhesive tape • a Stanley knife • a stencil brush (a round flat-ended brush)

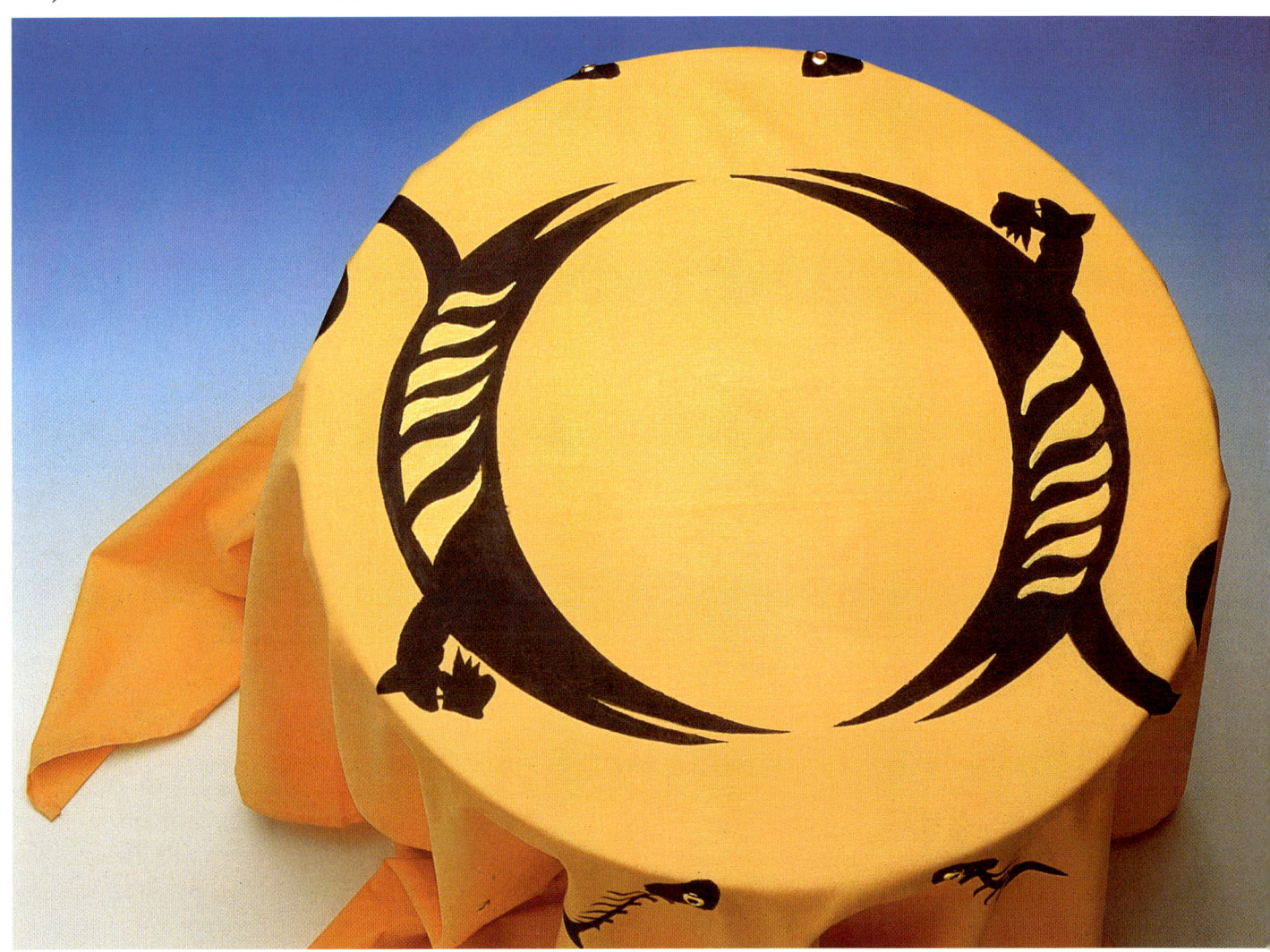

Snake velvet scarf

Not a feather boa, but a velvet boa for a touch of evening elegance.

Making up the snake

Use the dark brown velvet to form the body of the boa, and the beige velvet to make the head and the tail.

Photocopy the design for the head and the tail, increasing it to the necessary size. Place it on the beige velvet and cut each shape out twice, leaving about 1 centimetre extra around the edges for seams.

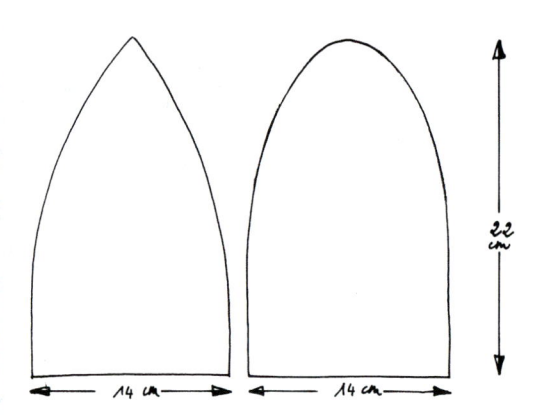

Cut two pieces for the inside of the mouth from the red taffeta. Place one piece of the red fabric on a velvet head piece, right sides together. Stitch around the red fabric, 1 centimetre from the edge, to 1 centimetre from the base. Turn inside out. Repeat for the other piece.

Assemble the two sections of the head, and the tail, and the rest of the body following the diagram.

Fold the boa in two lengthways, right sides together and stitch along the side, leaving the head open. Turn inside out.

Use the head opening to put kapok into the snake. Do not overstuff the snake.

Gently fill each side of the head with kapok.

Sew the two mouth ends of red taffeta together to close the opening.

Sew the two large beads on to the head to form the snake's eyes.

Finishing

If you wish to decorate the snake further, sew on lace or gold or iridescent beads. You can also make a string of beads that form a tongue for the snake, or sew some beads on to its tail.

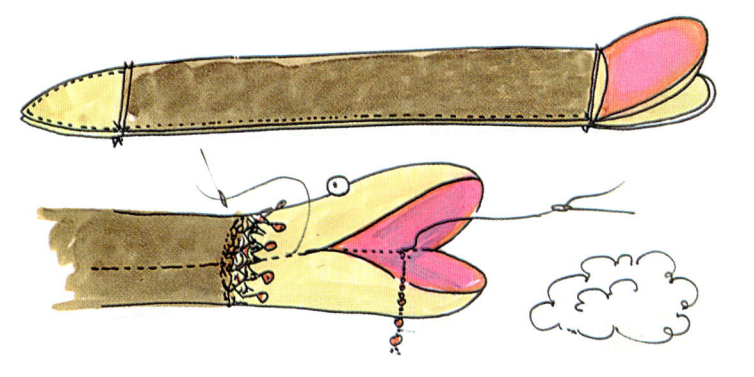

Materials

- a 30-centimetre piece of dark brown velvet, width 120 centimetres • a 30-centimetre piece of gold-beige velvet, width 120 centimetres • a 30-centimetre strip of red taffeta • kapok • two large pearly white beads • colourful beads, ribbon and lace for further embellishment

91

Photographic credits

Laurent Bessol/Muséum, Paris: 68-69, 69

Colibri: AM. Loubsens: 25b, 76b

Nature: Berthoule: 53a; Chaumeton: 46b, 49; Chaumeton/Berthoule: 74b; Chaumeton/Lanceau: 44a, 45, 54/55, 56c, 78b;
Chaumeton/Samba: 9b, 29a, 38a, 46a, 62c, 64b, 78a; Chaumeton/Varin: 58a; J.P. Ferrero: 28b, 28c, 67;
Gohier: 10a, 10b, 12b, 19, 28a, 34a, 34b, 35, 42b, 43, 61b, 62a, 66a, 76a; Grospas: 7, 8b, 20b, 47a, 47b, 59a, 65a, 65b;
Krasnodebski: 16a, 18a; Yves Lanceau: 10c (Miami Seaquarium), 14a, 14b, 16b, 18b, 18c, 26c, 30a, 30b,
31, 32, 33a, 34c, 44b, 52a, 52b, 53b, 56a, 56b, 57, 60b, 64a, 70c; Meitz: 15; Polking: 6-7, 21a, 21b, 26a, 26b, 27a,
29b, 48, 59b, 63, 70b, 71a, 72-73, 73, 75, 79a; Reille: 36a; F. Sauer: 8a, 8b, 13b, 33b, 58b, 60a, 66b, 70a, 71b, 74a;
R. Siegel: 17; Syvertsen: 27b

Okapia: I. Barth: 80a; Rolf Bender: 81a; Bildarchiv: 81b; T. Bledsoe: 80b; Raimund Cramm (1989): 37;
Marco Polo Film: 79b; Jeff Foott: 23; Johannes Gebbing: 12c; Christian Grzimek: 60c; Joe Mc Donald (1990): 41;
Jorge Provenza: 61a; Hans Reinhard: 39; Winfried Wisniewski: 77b; Konrad Wothe: 40, 78c

Phone: Deacon K./Auscape: 50a, 51; J.P. Ferrero: 24a, 42 a; J.P. Ferrero/J.M. Labat: 62b;
François Gohier: 11, 12a, 13a, 22a, 22b, 24b, 25a, 36b; C. Jardel/J.M. Labat: 38c; Parer & Parer-Cook/Auscape: 20a, 38b;
Mark Spencer/Auscape: 50b; Raymond Valter: 77a

Acknowledgements

The publishers would like to thank all those who have contributed to this book, in particular:
Evelyne-Alice Bridier, Antoine Caron, Michèle Forest, Nicolas Lemaire, Hervé Levano,
Marie-Cécile Moreau, Kha Luan Pham, Vincent Pompougnac,
Marie-Laure Sers-Besson, Emmanuelle Zumstein

Illustration: Franz Rey
Translation: Wendy Allatson for Ros Schwartz Translations - London, Sarah Snake